Voice Application Development for Android

A practical guide to develop advanced and exciting voice applications for Android using open source software

Michael F. McTear

Zoraida Callejas

PUBLISHING

BIRMINGHAM - MUMBAI

Voice Application Development for Android

First published: November 2013

Production Reference: 2041213

Published by Packt Publishing Ltd.
Livery Place
35 Livery Street
Birmingham B3 2PB, UK.

ISBN 978-1-78328-529-7

www.packtpub.com

Cover Image by Aniket Sawant (aniket_sawant_photography@hotmail.com)

Credits

Authors

Michael F. McTear

Zoraida Callejas

Reviewers

Deborah A. Dahl

Greg Milette

Acquisition Editor

Rebecca Youe

Commissioning Editor

Amit Ghodake

Technical Editors

Aparna Chand

Nadeem N. Bagban

Project Coordinator

Michelle Quadros

Proofreader

Hardip Sidhu

Indexer

Mehreen Deshmukh

Graphics

Ronak Dhruv

Production Coordinator

Aparna Bhagat

Cover Work

Aparna Bhagat

Foreword

There are many reasons why users need to speak and listen to mobile devices. We spend the first couple of years of our lives learning how to speak and listen to other people, so it is natural that we should be able to speak and listen to our mobile devices. As mobiles become smaller, the space available for physical keypads shrinks, making more difficult to use. Wearable devices such as Google Glass and smart watches don't have physical keypads. Speaking and listening is becoming a major means of interaction with mobile devices.

Eventually computers with microphones and speakers will be embedded into our home environment, eliminating the need for remote controls and handheld device. Speaking and listening will become the major form of communication with home appliances such as TVs, environmental controls, home security, coffee makers, ovens, and refrigerators.

When we perform tasks that require the use of our eyes and hands, we need speech technologies. Speech is the only practical way for interacting with an Android computer while driving a car or operating complex machinery. Holding and using a mobile device while driving is illegal in some places.

Siri and other intelligent agents enable mobile users to speak a search query. While these systems require sophisticated artificial intelligence and natural language techniques which are complex and time consuming to implement, they demonstrate the use of speech technologies that enable users to search for information.

Guides for "self-help" tasks requiring both hands and eyes present big opportunities for Android applications. Soon we will have electronic guides that speak and listen to help us assemble, troubleshoot, repair, fine-tune, and use equipment of all kinds. What's causing the strange sound in my car's engine? Why won't my television turn on? How do I adjust the air conditioner to cool the house? How do I fix a paper jam in my printer? Printed instructions, user guides, and manuals may be difficult to locate and difficult to read while your eyes are examining and your hands are manipulating the equipment.

Let a speech-enabled application talk you through the process, step-by-step. These self-help applications replace user documentation for almost any product.

Rather than hunting for the appropriate paperwork, just download the latest instructions simply by scanning the QR code on the product. After completing a step, simply say "next" to listen to the next instruction or "repeat" to hear the current instruction again. The self-help application can also display device schematics, illustrations, and even animations and video clips illustrating how to perform a task.

Voice messages and sounds are two of the best ways to catch a person's attention. Important alerts, notifications, and messages should be presented to the user vocally, in addition to displaying them on a screen where the user might not notice them.

These are a few of the many reasons to develop applications that speak and listen to users. This book will introduce you to building speech applications. Its examples at different levels of complexity are a good starting point for experimenting with this technology. Then for more ideas of interesting applications to implement, see the *Afterword* at the end of the book.

James A. Larson
Vice President and Founder of Larson Technical Services

About the Authors

Michael F. McTear is Emeritus Professor of Knowledge Engineering at the University of Ulster with a special research interest in spoken language technologies. He graduated in German Language and Literature from Queens University Belfast in 1965, was awarded MA in Linguistics at University of Essex in 1975, and a PhD at the University of Ulster in 1981. He has been Visiting Professor at the University of Hawaii (1986-87), the University of Koblenz, Germany (1994-95), and University of Granada, Spain (2006- 2010). He has been researching in the field of spoken dialogue systems for more than 15 years and is the author of the widely used text book *Spoken Dialogue Technology: Toward the Conversational User Interface (Springer Verlag, 2004)*. He also is a co-author of the book *Spoken Dialogue Systems (Morgan and Claypool, 2010)*.

Michael has delivered keynote addresses at many conferences and workshops, including the EU funded DUMAS Workshop, Geneva, 2004, the SIGDial workshop, Lisbon, 2005, the Spanish Conference on Natural Language Processing (SEPLN), Granada, 2005, and has delivered invited tutorials at IEEE/ ACL Conference on Spoken Language Technologies, Aruba, 2006, and ACL 2007, Prague. He has presented on several occasions at SpeechTEK, a conference for speech technology professionals, in New York and London. He is a certified VoiceXML developer and has taught VoiceXML at training courses to professionals from companies including Genesys, Oracle, Orange, 3, Fujitsu, and Santander. He was the main developer of the VoiceXML-based home monitoring system for patients with type-2 diabetes, currently in use at the Ulster Hospital, Northern Ireland.

Zoraida Callejas is Assistant Professor at the University of Granada, Spain, where she has been teaching several subjects related to Oral and Multimodal Interfaces, Object Oriented Programming, and Software Engineering for the last eight years. She graduated in Computer Science in 2005, and was awarded a PhD in 2008 from the University of Granada. She has been Visiting Professor in Technical University of Liberec, Czech Republic (2007-13), University of Trento, Italy (2008), University of Ulster, Northern Ireland (2009), Technical University of Berlin, Germany (2010), University of Ulm, Germany (2012), and Telecom ParisTech, France (2013).

Zoraida focuses her research on speech technology and in particular, on spoken and multimodal dialogue systems. Zoraida has made presentations at the main conferences in the area of dialogue systems, and has published her research in several international journals and books. She has also coordinated training courses in the development of interactive speech processing systems, and has regularly taught object-oriented software development in Java in different graduate courses for nine years. Currently, she leads a local project for the development of Android speech applications for intellectually disabled users.

Acknowledgement

We would like to acknowledge the advice and help provided by Amit Ghodake, our Commissioning Editor at Packt Publishing, as well as the support of Michelle Quadros, our Project Coordinator, who ensured that we kept to schedule. A special thanks to our technical reviewers, Deborah A. Dahl and Greg Milette, whose comments and careful reading of the first draft of the book enabled us to make numerous changes in the final version that have greatly improved the quality of the book.

Finally, we would like to acknowledge our partners Sandra McTear and David Griol for putting up with our absences while we devoted so much of our time to writing, and sharing the stress of our tight schedule.

About the Reviewers

Dr. Deborah A. Dahl has been working in the areas of speech and natural language processing technologies for over 30 years. She received a Ph.D. in linguistics from the University of Minnesota in 1983, followed by a post-doctoral fellowship in Cognitive Science at the University of Pennsylvania. At Unisys Corporation, she performed research on natural language understanding and spoken dialog systems, and led teams which used these technologies in government and commercial applications. Dr. Dahl founded her company, Conversational Technologies, in 2002. Conversational Technologies provides expertise in the state of the art of speech, natural language, and multimodal technologies through reports, analysis, training, and design services that enable its clients to apply these technologies in creating compelling mobile, desktop, and cloud solutions. Dr. Dahl has published over 50 technical papers, and is the editor of the book *Practical Spoken Dialog Systems*. She is also a frequent speaker at speech industry conferences. In addition to her technical work, Dr. Dahl is active in the World Wide Web Consortium, working on standards development for speech and multimodal interaction as chair of the Multimodal Interaction Working Group. She received the 2012 Speech Luminary Award from Speech Technology Magazine. This is an annual award honoring individuals who push the boundaries of the speech technology industry, and, in doing so, influence others in a significant way.

Greg Milette is a programmer, author, entrepreneur, musician, and father of two who loves implementing great ideas. He has been developing Android apps since 2009 when he released a voice controlled recipe app called Digital Recipe Sidekick. In between yapping to his Android device in the kitchen, Greg co-authored a comprehensive book on sensors and speech recognition called *Professional Android Sensor Programming*, published by Wiley in 2012 and founded a mobile app consulting company called Gradison Technologies, Inc. He acknowledges the contributions to his work from the Android community, and his family who tirelessly review and test his material and constantly refresh his office with happiness.

www.PacktPub.com

Support files, eBooks, discount offers and more

You might want to visit www.PacktPub.com for support files and downloads related to your book.

Did you know that Packt offers eBook versions of every book published, with PDF and ePub files available? You can upgrade to the eBook version at www.PacktPub.com and as a print book customer, you are entitled to a discount on the eBook copy. Get in touch with us at service@packtpub.com for more details.

At www.PacktPub.com, you can also read a collection of free technical articles, sign up for a range of free newsletters and receive exclusive discounts and offers on Packt books and eBooks.

http://PacktLib.PacktPub.com

Do you need instant solutions to your IT questions? PacktLib is Packt's online digital book library. Here, you can access, read and search across Packt's entire library of books.

Why Subscribe?

- Fully searchable across every book published by Packt
- Copy and paste, print and bookmark content
- On demand and accessible via web browser

Free Access for Packt account holders

If you have an account with Packt at www.PacktPub.com, you can use this to access PacktLib today and view nine entirely free books. Simply use your login credentials for immediate access.

Table of Contents

Preface	**1**
Chapter 1: Speech on Android Devices	**7**
Using speech on an Android device	**7**
Speech-to-text	7
Text-to-speech	8
Voice Search	8
Android Voice Actions	8
Virtual Personal Assistants	9
Designing and developing a speech app	**11**
Why Google speech?	**11**
What is needed to create a Virtual Personal Assistant?	**12**
Summary	**14**
Chapter 2: Text-to-Speech Synthesis	**15**
Introducing text-to-speech synthesis	**15**
The technology of text-to-speech synthesis	**16**
Using pre-recorded speech instead of TTS	**17**
Using Google text-to-speech synthesis	**17**
Starting the TTS engine	18
Developing applications with Google TTS	**19**
TTSWithLib app – Reading user input	19
TTSReadFile app – Reading a file out loud	20
Summary	**21**
Chapter 3: Speech Recognition	**23**
The technology of speech recognition	**23**
Using Google speech recognition	**24**

Developing applications with the Google speech recognition API	**25**
ASRWithIntent app	26
ASRWithLib app	31
Summary	**34**
Chapter 4: Simple Voice Interactions	**35**
Voice interactions	**35**
VoiceSearch app	**36**
VoiceLaunch app	**37**
VoiceSearchConfirmation app	**43**
Summary	**44**
Chapter 5: Form-filling Dialogs	**47**
Form-filling dialogs	**47**
Implementing form-filling dialogs	**48**
Threading	**49**
XMLLib	**50**
FormFillLib	**51**
VXMLParser	52
DialogInterpreter	53
MusicBrain app	**55**
Summary	**58**
Chapter 6: Grammars for Dialog	**61**
Grammars for speech recognition and natural language understanding	**61**
NLU with hand-crafted grammars	**62**
Statistical NLU	**66**
NLULib	68
Processing XML grammars	68
Processing statistical grammars	71
The GrammarTest app	**72**
Summary	**73**
Chapter 7: Multilingual and Multimodal Dialogs	**75**
Multilinguality	**75**
Multimodality	**78**
Summary	**85**
Chapter 8: Dialogs with Virtual Personal Assistants	**87**
The technology of VPA	**87**
Determining the user's intention	88
Making an appropriate response	**90**

Pandorabots **90**
AIML 91
Using oob tag to add additional functions 93
The VPALib library **94**
Creating a Pandorabot **95**
Sample VPAs – Jack, Derek, and Stacy **96**
Alternative approaches 98
Summary **99**
Chapter 9: Taking it Further **101**
Developing a more advanced Virtual Personal Assistant **101**
Summary **103**
Afterword **105**
Index **107**

Preface

The idea of being able to talk with a computer has fascinated many people for a long time. However, until recently, this has seemed to be the stuff of science fiction. Now things have changed so that people who own a smartphone or tablet can perform many tasks on their device using voice — you can send a text message, update your calendar, set an alarm, and ask the sorts of queries that you would previously have typed into your search box. Often voice input is more convenient, especially on small devices where physical limitations make typing and tapping more difficult.

This book provides a practical guide to the development of voice apps for Android devices, using the Google Speech APIs for text-to-speech (TTS) and automated speech recognition (ASR) as well as other open source software. Although there are many books that cover Android programming in general, there is no single source that deals comprehensively with the development of voice-based applications for Android.

Developing for a voice user interface shares many of the characteristics of developing for more traditional interfaces, but there are also ways in which voice application development has its own specific requirements and it is important that developers coming to this area are aware of common pitfalls and difficulties. This book provides some introductory material to cover those aspects that may not be familiar to professionals from a mainstream computing background. It then goes on to show in detail how to put together complete apps, beginning with simple programs and progressing to more sophisticated applications. By building on the examples in the book and experimenting with the techniques described, you will be able to bring the power of voice to your Android apps, making them smarter and more intuitive, and boosting your users' mobile experience.

What this book covers

Chapter 1, Speech on Android Devices, discusses how speech can be used on Android devices and outlines the technologies involved.

Chapter 2, Text-to-Speech Synthesis, covers the technology of text-to-speech synthesis and how to use the Google TTS engine.

Chapter 3, Speech Recognition, provides an overview of the technology of speech recognition and how to use the Google Speech to Text engine.

Chapter 4, Simple Voice Interactions, shows how to build simple interactions in which the user and app can talk to each other to retrieve some information or perform an action.

Chapter 5, Form-filling Dialogs, illustrates how to create voice-enabled dialogs that are similar to form-filling in a traditional web application.

Chapter 6, Grammars for Dialog, introduces the use of grammars to interpret inputs from the user that go beyond single words and phrases.

Chapter 7, Multilingual and Multimodal Dialogs, looks at how to build apps that use different languages and modalities.

Chapter 8, Dialogs with Virtual Personal Assistants, shows how to build a speech-enabled personal assistant.

Chapter 9, Taking it Further, shows how to develop a more advanced Virtual Personal Assistant.

What you need for this book

To run the code examples and develop your own apps, you will need to install the Android SDK and platform tools. A complete bundle that includes the essential Android SDK component and a version of the Eclipse IDE with built-in ADT (Android Developer Tools) along with tutorials is available for download at `http://developer.android.com/sdk/`.

You will also need an Android device to build and test the examples as Android ASR (speech recognition) does not work on virtual devices (emulators).

Who this book is for

This book is intended for all those who are interested in speech application development, including students of speech technology and mobile computing. We assume some background of programming in general, particularly in Java. We also assume some familiarity with Android programming.

Conventions

In this book, you will find a number of styles of text that distinguish between different kinds of information. Here are some examples of these styles, and an explanation of their meaning.

Code words in text, database table names, folder names, filenames, file extensions, pathnames, dummy URLs, user input, and Twitter handles are shown as follows: "The following lines of code create a `TextToSpeech` object that implements the `onInit` method of the `onInitListener` interface."

A block of code is set as follows:

```
TextToSpeech tts = new TextToSpeech(this, new OnInitListener(){
    public void onInit(int status){
        if (status == TextToSpeech.SUCCESS)
            speak("Hello world", TextToSpeech.QUEUE_ADD, null);
    }
}
```

When we wish to draw your attention to a particular part of a code block, the relevant lines or items are set in bold:

```
Interpret field i:
        Play prompt of field i
        Listen for ASR result
        Process ASR result:
                If the recognition was successful, then save recognized
                keyword as value for the field i and move to the next field
                If there was a no match or no input, then interpret field i
                If there is any other error, then stop interpreting
Move to the next field:
        If the next field has already a value assigned, then move to
        the next one
        If the last field in the form is reached,
        thenendOfDialogue=true
```

New terms and important words are shown in bold. Words that you see on the screen, in menus or dialog boxes for example, appear in the text like this: "**Please say a word of the album title**."

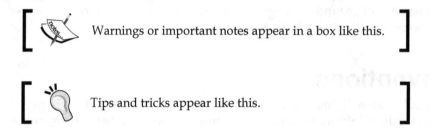

Warnings or important notes appear in a box like this.

Tips and tricks appear like this.

Reader feedback

Feedback from our readers is always welcome. Let us know what you think about this book—what you liked or may have disliked. Reader feedback is important for us to develop titles that you really get the most out of.

To send us general feedback, simply send an e-mail to feedback@packtpub.com, and mention the book title via the subject of your message.

If there is a topic that you have expertise in and you are interested in either writing or contributing to a book, see our author guide on www.packtpub.com/authors.

Customer support

Now that you are the proud owner of a Packt book, we have a number of things to help you to get the most from your purchase.

Downloading the example code

You can download the example code files for all Packt books you have purchased from your account at http://www.packtpub.com. If you purchased this book elsewhere, you can visit http://www.packtpub.com/support and register to have the files e-mailed directly to you.

Web page for the book

There is a web page for the book at http://lsi.ugr.es/zoraida/androidspeechbook, with additional resources, including ideas for exercises and projects, suggestions for further reading, and links to useful web pages.

Errata

Although we have taken every care to ensure the accuracy of our content, mistakes do happen. If you find a mistake in one of our books—maybe a mistake in the text or the code—we would be grateful if you would report this to us. By doing so, you can save other readers from frustration and help us improve subsequent versions of this book. If you find any errata, please report them by visiting http://www.packtpub.com/ submit-errata, selecting your book, clicking on the **errata submission form** link, and entering the details of your errata. Once your errata are verified, your submission will be accepted and the errata will be uploaded on our website, or added to any list of existing errata, under the Errata section of that title. Any existing errata can be viewed by selecting your title from http://www.packtpub.com/support.

Piracy

Piracy of copyright material on the Internet is an ongoing problem across all media. At Packt, we take the protection of our copyright and licenses very seriously. If you come across any illegal copies of our works, in any form, on the Internet, please provide us with the location address or website name immediately so that we can pursue a remedy.

Please contact us at copyright@packtpub.com with a link to the suspected pirated material.

We appreciate your help in protecting our authors, and our ability to bring you valuable content.

Questions

You can contact us at questions@packtpub.com if you are having a problem with any aspect of the book, and we will do our best to address it.

1
Speech on Android Devices

Have you ever wanted to create voice-based apps that you could run on your own Android device; apps that you could talk to and that could talk back to you? This chapter provides an introduction to the use of speech on Android devices, using open-source APIs from Google for text-to-speech synthesis and speech recognition. Following a brief overview of the world of **Voice User Interfaces (VUIs)**, the chapter outlines the components of an interactive voice application (or virtual personal assistant).

By the end of this chapter you should have a good understanding of what is required to create a voice-based app using freely available resources from Google.

Using speech on an Android device

Android devices provide built-in speech-to-text and text-to-speech capabilities. The following are some examples of speech-based apps on Android:

Speech-to-text

With speech-to-text users of Android devices can dictate into any text box on the device where textual input is required, for example, e-mail, text messaging, and search. The keyboard control contains a button with a microphone symbol and two letters indicating the language input settings, which can be changed by the user. On pressing the microphone button a window pops up asking the user to **Speak Now**. The spoken input is automatically transcribed into written text. The user can then decide what to do with the transcribed text.

Accuracy rates have improved considerably for dictation on small devices, on one hand due to the use of large-scale cloud-based resources for speech recognition, and on the other, to the fact that the device is usually held close to the user's mouth so that a more reliable acoustic signal can be obtained. One of the main challenges for voice dictation is that the input is unpredictable—users can say literally anything—and so a large general vocabulary is required to cover all possible inputs. Other challenges include dealing with background noise, sloppy speech, and unfamiliar accents.

Text-to-speech

Text-to-speech (TTS) is used to convert text to speech. Various applications can take advantage of TTS. For example, TalkBack, which is available through the Accessibility option, uses TTS to help blind and visually impaired users by describing what items are touched, selected and activated. TalkBack can also be used to read a book in the Google Play Books app. The TTS function is also available on Android Kindle as well as on Google Maps for giving step-by-step driving instructions. There is a wide range of third-party apps that make use of TTS, and alternative TTS engines are also available.

Voice Search

Voice Search provides the same functionality on Android devices as the traditional Google Search except that instead of typing a query the user speaks it. Voice Search is available using the microphone in the Google Search widget. In Voice Search the recognized text is passed to the search engine and executed in the same way that a typed query is executed.

A new feature of Voice Search is that, in addition to returning a list of links, a spoken response to the query is returned. For example, in response to the question "How tall is the Eiffel tower?", the app replies, "The Eiffel tower is 324 meters tall." It is also possible to ask follow-up questions using pronouns, for example, "When was it built?". This additional functionality is made possible by combining Google's Knowledge Graph—a knowledge base used by Google—with its conversational search technology to provide a more conversational style of interaction.

Android Voice Actions

Android Voice Actions can also be accessed using the microphone in the Google Search widget. Voice Actions allow the user to control their device using voice commands. Voice Actions require input that matches a particular structure, as shown in the following list from Google's webpage: `http://www.google.co.uk/intl/en_uk/mobile/voice-actions/`. Note: items with * are optional. Italicized items are the words to be spoken.

Voice Action	Structure	Example
Send text messages	send text to [recipient] [message]*	send text to Allison Miller Running late. I will be home around 9
Call businesses	call [business name] [location]*	call Soho Pizzeria London
View a map	map of [address/city]	map of London
Search Google	[your query]	pictures of Stonehenge at sunset
Get directions	navigate to [address/city/ business name]	navigate to British Museum London or navigate to 24 Mill Street
Call contacts	call [contact name] [phone type]*	call Allison Miller home
Go to websites	go to [website]	go to Wikipedia

The structures in Voice Actions allow them to be mapped on to actions that are available on the device. For example, the keyword **call** indicates a phone call while the key phrase **go to** indicates a website to be launched. Additional processing is required to extract the parameters of the actions, such as **contact name** and **website**.

Virtual Personal Assistants

One of the most exciting speech-based apps is the Virtual Personal Assistant (VPA), which acts like a personal assistant, performing a range of tasks such as finding information about local restaurants; carrying out commands involving apps on the device, for example, using speech to set the alarm or update the calendar; and engaging in general conversation. There are at least 20 VPAs available for Android devices (see the web page for this book) although the best-known VPA is Siri, which has been available on the iPhone iOS since 2011. You can find examples of interactions with Siri that are similar to those performed by Android VPAs on Apple's website http://www.apple.com/uk/ios/siri/. Many VPAs, including Siri, have been created with a personality and an ability to respond in a humorous way to trick questions and dubious input, thus adding to their entertainment value. See examples at http://www.sirifunny.com as well as numerous video clips on YouTube.

It is worth mentioning that a number of technologies share some of the characteristics of VPAs as explained in the following:

Dialog systems, which have a long tradition in academic research, are based on the vision of developing systems that can communicate with humans in natural language (initially written text but more recently speech). The first systems were concerned with obtaining information, for example, flight times or stock quotes. The next generation enabled users to engage in some form of transaction, in banking or making a travel reservation, while more recent systems are being developed to assist in troubleshooting, for example, guiding a user who is having difficulty setting up some item of equipment. A wide range of techniques have been used to implement dialog systems, including rule-based and statistically-based dialog processing.

Voice User Interfaces (**VUIs**), which are similar to dialog systems but with the emphasis on commercial deployment. Here the focus has tended to be on systems for specific purposes, such as call routing, directory assistance, and transactional dialogs for example, travel, hotel, flight, car rental, or bank balance. Many current VUIs have been designed using VoiceXML, a markup language based on XML. The VoiceXML scripts are then interpreted on a voice browser that also provides the required speech and telephony functions.

Chatbots, which have been used traditionally to simulate human conversation. The earliest chatbots go back to the 1960s with the famous ELIZA program written by Joseph Weizenbaum that simulated a Rogerian psychotherapist—often in a convincing way. More recently chatbots have been used in education, information retrieval, business, e-commerce, and in automated help desks. Chatbots use a sophisticated pattern-matching algorithm to match the user's input and to retrieve appropriate responses. Most chatbots have been text-based although increasingly speech-based chatbots are beginning to emerge (see further in *Chapter 8, Dialogs with Virtual Personal Assistants*).

Embodied conversational agents (**ECAs**), are computer-generated animated characters that combine facial expression, body stance, hand gestures, and speech to provide an enriched channel of communication. By enhancing the visual dimensions of face-to-face interaction embodied conversational agents can appear more trustworthy and believable, and also more interesting and entertaining. Embodied conversational agents have been used in applications such as interactive language learning, virtual training environments, virtual reality game shows, and interactive fiction and storytelling systems. Increasingly they are being used in e-commerce and e-banking to provide friendly and helpful automated help. See, for example, the agent Anna at the IKEA website `http://www.ikea.com/gb/en/`.

Virtual Personal Assistants differ from these technologies in that they allow users to use speech to perform many of the functions that are available on mobile devices, such as sending a text message, consulting and updating the calendar, or setting an alarm. They also provide access to web services, such as finding a restaurant, tracking a delivery, booking a flight, or using information services such as Knowledge Graph, Wolfram Alpha, or Wikipedia. Because they have access to contextual information on the device such as the user's location, time and date, contacts, and calendar, the VPA can provide information such as restaurant recommendations relevant to the user's location and preferences.

Designing and developing a speech app

Speech app design shares many of the characteristics of software design in general, but there are also some aspects unique to voice interfaces — for example, dealing with the issue that speech recognition is always going to be less than 100 percent accurate, and so is less reliable compared with input when using a GUI. Another issue is that, since speech is transient, especially on devices with no visual display, greater demands are put on the user's memory compared with a GUI app.

There are many factors that contribute to the usability of a speech-based app. It is important to perform extensive use case analysis in order to determine the requirements of the system, looking at issues such as whether the app is to replace or complement an existing app; whether speech is appropriate as a medium for input/output; the type of service to be provided by the app; the types of user who will make use of the app; and the general deployment environment for the app.

Why Google speech?

The following are our reasons for using Google speech:

- **The proliferation of Android devices**: Recent information on Android states that "Android had a worldwide smartphone market share of 75% during the third quarter of 2012,with 750 million devices activated in total and 1.5 million activations per day." (From `http://www.idc.com/getdoc.jsp?containerId=prUS23771812 Retrieved 09/07/2013`).

- **The Android SDK is open source**: The fact that the Android SDK is open source makes it more easily available for developers and enthusiasts to create apps, compared with some other operating systems. Anyone can develop their own apps using a free development environment such as Eclipse and then upload it to their Android device for their own personal use and enjoyment.

- **The Google Speech APIs**: The Google Speech APIs are available for free for use on Android devices. This means that the Speech APIs are useful for developers wishing to try out speech without investing in expensive commercially available alternatives. As Google employs many of the top speech scientists, their speech APIs are comparable in performance to those on offer commercially.

You may also try...

Nuance NDEV Mobile, which supports a number of languages for text-to-speech synthesis and speech recognition as well as providing a PhoneGap plug-in to enable developers to implement their apps on different platforms (`http://dragonmobile.nuancemobiledeveloper.com`).

The AT&T Speech Mashup (`http://www.research.att.com/projects/SpeechMashup/`), which supports the development of speech-based apps and the use of W3C standard speech recognition grammars.

What is needed to create a Virtual Personal Assistant?

The following figure shows the various components required to build a speech-enabled VPA.

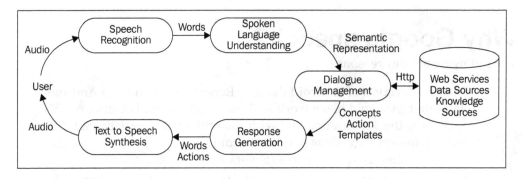

A basic requirement for a VPA is that it should be able to speak and to understand speech. Text to speech synthesis, which provides the ability to speak, is discussed in *Chapter 2, Text To Speech Synthesis*, while speech recognition is covered in *Chapter 3, Speech Recognition*. However, while these capabilities are fundamental for a voice-enabled assistant, they are not sufficient. The ability to engage in dialog and connect to web services and device functions is also required as the basis of personal assistance. To do these things a VPA requires the following:

- A method for controlling the dialog, determining who should take the dialog initiative and what topics they should cover. In practice this can be simplified by having one-shot interactions in which the user simply speaks their query and the app responds. One-shot interactions are covered in *Chapter 4, Simple Voice Interactions*. System-directed dialogs, in which the app asks a series of questions — as in web-based form-filling (for example, to book a hotel or rent a car), are covered in *Chapter 5, Form-filling Dialogs*.

- A method for interpreting the user's input once it has been recognized. This is the task of the Spoken Language Understanding component which, among other things, provides a semantic interpretation representing the meaning of what the user said. Since in many commercial systems input is restricted to single words or phrases, the interpretation is relatively straightforward. Two different approaches will be illustrated in *Chapter 6, Grammars for Dialog*: how to create a hand-crafted grammar that covers the words and phrases that the user might say; and how to use statistical grammars to cover a wider range of inputs and to provide a more robust interpretation. It also provides different modalities if speech input and output is not possible or performance is poor. A VPA should also have the ability to use different languages, if required. These topics are covered in *Chapter 7, Multilingual and Multimodal Dialogs*.

- Determining relevant actions and generating appropriate responses. These aspects of dialog management and response generation are described in *Chapter 7, Multilingual and Multimodal Dialogs*, and in *Chapter 8, Dialogs with Personal Virtual Assistants*.

Building on the basic technologies of text-to-speech synthesis and speech recognition, as presented in Chapter 2 and Chapter 3, Chapters 4-8 cover a range of techniques that will enable developers to take the basic technologies further and create speech-based apps using the Google speech APIs.

Summary

This chapter has provided an introduction to speech technology on Android devices. We examined various types of speech app that are currently available on Android devices. We also looked at why we decided to focus on Google Speech APIs as tools for the developer. Finally we introduced the main technologies required to create a Virtual Personal Assistant. These technologies will be covered in the remaining chapters of this book.

We will introduce you to text-to-speech synthesis (TTS) and show how to use the Google TTS API to develop applications that speak in the next chapter.

2
Text-to-Speech Synthesis

Have you ever wondered how your mobile device can read aloud your favorite e-book or your last e-mail? In this chapter, you will learn about the technology of text-to-speech synthesis (TTS) and how to use the Google TTS engine to develop applications that speak. The topics covered are:

- The technology of text to speech synthesis
- Google text to speech synthesis
- Developing applications using text to speech synthesis

By the end of this chapter, you should be able to develop apps that use text-to-speech synthesis on Android devices.

Introducing text-to-speech synthesis

Text-to-speech synthesis, often abbreviated to TTS, is a technology that enables a written text to be converted into speech. TTS has been used widely to provide screen reading for people with visual impairments, and also for users with severe speech impairments. Perhaps the best known user of speech synthesis technology is the physicist Stephen Hawking who suffers from motor neurone disease and uses TTS as his speech has become unintelligible. With the aid of word prediction technology he is able to construct a sentence which he then sends to the built-in TTS system (see further: `http://www.hawking.org.uk/the-computer.html`).

TTS is also used widely in situations where the user's hands or eyes are busy, for example, while driving navigation systems speak the directions as the vehicle progresses along a route. Another widespread use for TTS is in public announcement systems, for example, at airports or train stations. TTS is also used in phone-based call-center applications and in spoken dialog systems in general to speak the system's prompts, and in conjunction with talking heads on websites that use conversational agents to provide customer help and support.

The quality of a TTS system has a significant bearing on how it is perceived by users. Users may be annoyed by a system that sounds robotic or that pronounces words such as names or addresses incorrectly. However, as long as the output from the TTS is intelligible, this should at least allow the system to perform adequately.

The technology of text-to-speech synthesis

There are two main stages in text-to-speech synthesis:

- Text analysis, where the text to be synthesized is analyzed and prepared for spoken output.
- Wave form generation, where the analyzed text is converted into speech.

There can be many problems in the text analysis stage. For example, what is the correct pronunciation of the word *staring*? Is it to be based on the combination of the word *star + ing* or of *stare + ing*? Determining the answer to this question involves complex analysis of the structure of words; in this case, determining how the root form of a word such as *stare* is changed by the addition of a suffix such as *ing*.

There are also words that have alternative pronunciations depending on their use in a particular sentence. For example, *live* as a verb will rhyme with *give*, but as an adjective it rhymes with *five*. The part of speech also affects stress assignment within a word; for example, *record* as a noun is pronounced *'record* (with the stress on the first syllable), and as a verb as *re'cord* (with the stress on the second syllable).

Another problem concerns the translation of numeric values into a form suitable for spoken output (referred to as *normalization*). For example, the item *12.9.13*, if it represents a date, should not be spoken out as *twelve dot nine dot thirteen* but as *December 9th, two thousand thirteen*. Note that application developers using the Google TTS API do not have to concern themselves with these issues as they are built in to the TTS engine.

Turning to wave form generation, the main methods used in earlier systems were either **articulatory synthesis**, which attempts to model the physical process by which humans produce speech, or **formant synthesis**, which models characteristics of the acoustic signal.

Nowadays **concatenative speech synthesis** is used, in which pre-recorded units of speech are stored in a speech database and selected and joined together during speech generation. The units are of various sizes; single sounds (or phones), adjacent pairs of sounds (diphones), which produce a more natural output since the pronunciation of a phone varies based on the surrounding phones; syllables, words, phrases, and sentences; and complex algorithms have been developed to select the best chain of candidate units and to join them together smoothly to produce fluent speech. The output of some systems is often indistinguishable from real human speech, particularly where prosody is used effectively. Prosody includes phrasing, pitch, loudness, tempo, and rhythm, and is used to convey differences in meaning as well as attitude.

Using pre-recorded speech instead of TTS

Although the quality of TTS has improved considerably over the past few years, many commercial enterprises prefer to use pre-recorded speech in order to guarantee high-quality output. Professional artists, often referred to as voice talent, are employed to record the system's prompts.

The downside of pre-recorded prompts is that they cannot be used where the text to be output is unpredictable — as in apps for reading e-mail, text messages, or news, or in applications where new names are being continually added to the customer list. Even where the text can be predicted but involves a large number of combinations — as in flight announcements at airports — the different elements of the output have to be concatenated from pre-recorded segments but in many cases the result is jerky and unnatural. Another situation is where output in other languages might be made available. It would be possible to employ voice talent to record the output in the various languages but for greater flexibility the use of different language versions of the TTS might be less costly and sufficient for purpose.

There has been a considerable amount of research on the issue of TTS versus pre-recorded speech. See, for example, *Practical Speech User Interface Design* by *James R. Lewis, CRC Press*.

Using Google text-to-speech synthesis

TTS has been available on Android devices since Android 1.6 (API Level 4).The components of the Google TTS API (package android.speech.tts) are documented at http://developer.android.com/reference/android/speech/tts/package-summary.html. Interfaces and classes are listed and further details can be obtained by clicking on these.

Starting the TTS engine

Starting the TTS engine involves creating an instance of the TextToSpeech class along with the method that will be executed when the TTS engine is initialized. Checking that TTS has been initialized is done through an interface called OnInitListener. If TTS initialization is complete, the method onInit is invoked.

The following lines of code create a TextToSpeech object that implements the onInit method of the onInitListener interface.

```
TextToSpeech tts = new TextToSpeech(this, new OnInitListener(){
    public void onInit(int status){
        if (status == TextToSpeech.SUCCESS)
            speak("Hello world", TextToSpeech.QUEUE_ADD, null);
    }
}
```

Downloading the example code

You can download the example code files for all Packt books you have purchased from your account at http://www.packtpub.com. If you purchased this book elsewhere, you can visit http://www.packtpub.com/support and register to have the files e-mailed directly to you.

You can also visit the web page for the book: http://lsi.ugr.es/zoraida/androidspeechbook

In the example, when TTS is initialized correctly, the speak method is invoked, which may include the following parameters:

- QUEUE_ADD: The new entry placed at the end of the playback queue.
- QUEUE_FLUSH: All entries in the playback queue are dropped and replaced by the new entry.

Due to limited storage on some devices, not all languages that are supported may actually be installed on a particular device. For this reason, it is important to check if a particular language is available before creating the TextToSpeech object. This way, it is possible to download and install the required language-specific resource files if necessary. This is done by sending an Intent with the action ACTION_CHECK_TTS_DATA method, which is part of the TextToSpeech.Engine class as given in the following code:

```
Intent intent = new
    Intent(TextToSpeech.Engine.ACTION_CHECK_TTS_DATA);
startActivityForResult(intent,TTS_DATA_CHECK);
```

If the language data has been correctly installed, the onActivityResult handler will receive a CHECK_VOICE_DATA_PASS, this is when we should create the TextToSpeech instance. If the data is not available, the action ACTION_INSTALL_TTS_DATA will be executed as given in the following code:

```
Intent installData = new Intent (Engine.ACTION_INSTALL_TTS_DATA);
startActivity(installData);
```

You can see the complete code in the TTSWithIntent app available in the code bundle.

Developing applications with Google TTS

In order to avoid repeating the code in several places, and to be able to focus on the new parts as we progress to more complex applications, we have encapsulated the most frequently used TTS functionalities into a library named TTSLib (see sandra. libs.tts in the source code), which is employed in the different applications.

The TTS.java class has been created following the Singleton design pattern. This means that there can only be a single instance of this class, and thus an app that employs the library uses a single TTS object with which all messages are synthesized. This has multiple advantages, such as optimizing resources and preventing developers from unwittingly creating multiple TextToSpeech instances within the same application.

TTSWithLib app – Reading user input

The next figure shows the opening screen of this app, in which the user types a text, chooses a language, and then presses a button to make the device start or stop reading the text. By default, the option checked is the default language in the device as shown in the following screenshot:

The code in the `TTSWithLib.java` file mainly initializes the elements in the visual user interface and controls the language chosen (`setLocaleList` method), as well as what to do when the users presses the **Speak** (`setSpeakButton`) and **Stop** (`setStopButton`) buttons. As can be observed in the code shown, the main functionality is to invoke the corresponding methods in the `TTS.java` file from the `TTSLib` library. In `TTS.java` (see the `TTSLib` project in the code bundle) there are three methods named `setLocale` for establishing the locale. The first one receives two arguments corresponding to the language and the country codes. For example, for British English the language code is `EN` and the country code `GB`, whereas for American English they are `EN` and `US` respectively. The second method sets the language code only. The third method does not receive any argument and just sets the device's default language. As can be observed, if any argument is null in the first or second method, then the second and third methods are invoked.

The other important methods are responsible for starting (the `speak` method) and stopping (the `stop` method) the synthesis, whereas the `shutdown` method releases the native resources used by the TTS engine. It is good practice to invoke the `shutdown` method, we do it in the `onDestroy` method of the calling activities; for example, in the `TTSDemo.java` file).

TTSReadFile app – Reading a file out loud

A more realistic scenario for text-to-speech synthesis is to read out some text, especially when the user's eyes and hands are busy. Similar to the previous example, the app retrieves some text and the user presses the **Speak** button to hear it. A **Stop** button is provided in case the user does not wish to hear all of the text.

A potential use-case for this type of app is when the user accesses some text on the web; for example, a news item, an e-mail, or a sports report. To do this would involve additional code to access the internet and this goes beyond the scope of the current app (see for example, the MusicBrain app in *Chapter 5, Form-filling Dialogs*). So, to keep matters simple, the text is pre-stored in the `Assets` folder and retrieved from there. It is left as an exercise for the reader to retrieve texts from other sources and pass them to TTS to be read out. The following screenshot shows the opening screen:

The file `TTSReadFile.java` is similar to the file `TTSWithLib.java`. As shown in the code, the main difference is that it uses English as the default language (as it matches the stored file) and obtains the text from a file instead of from the user interface (see the `onClickListener` method for the `speakbutton`, and the `getText` method in the code bundle).

> There are several more advanced issues discussed in detail in the book: *Professional Android™ Sensor Programming, Greg Milette and Adam Stroud, Wrox, Chapter 16*. There are methods for selecting different voices, depending on what is available on particular devices. For example, the TTS API provides additional methods to help you play back different types of text.

Summary

This chapter has shown how to use the Google TTS API to implement text to speech synthesis on a device. An overview of the technology behind text to speech synthesis was provided, followed by an introduction to the elements of the Google TTS API. Two examples were presented illustrating the basics of text-to-speech synthesis. In subsequent chapters more sophisticated approaches will be developed.

The next chapter deals with the other side of the speech coin: speech-to-text (or speech recognition).

3
Speech Recognition

Have you ever tapped through several menus and options on your device until you were able to do what you wanted? Have you ever wished you could just say some words and make it work? This chapter looks at **Automatic Speech Recognition (ASR)**, the process that converts spoken words to written text. The topics covered are as follows:

- The technology of speech recognition
- Using Google speech recognition
- Developing applications with the Google speech recognition API

By the end of this chapter, you should have a good understanding of the issues involved in using speech recognition in an app and should be able to develop simple apps using the Google speech API.

The technology of speech recognition

The following are the two main stages in speech recognition:

- **Signal processing**: This stage involves capturing the words spoken into a microphone and using an **analogue-to-digital converter** (**ADC**) to translate it into digital data that can be processed by the computer. The ADC processes the digital data to remove noise and perform other processes such as echo cancellation in order to be able to extract those features that are relevant for speech recognition.
- **Speech recognition**: The signal is split into minute segments that are matched against the phonemes of the language to be recognized. Phonemes are the smallest unit of speech, roughly equivalent to the letters of the alphabet. For example, the phonemes in the word cat are /k/, /æ/, and /t/. In English, for example, there are around 40 phonemes, depending on which variety of English is being spoken.

The most successful approach to speech recognition has been to model speech statistically so that the outcome of the process is a series of guesses (or hypotheses) as to what the user might have said, ranked according to the computed probability. Complex probabilistic functions are used to perform this statistical modeling. The most commonly used among these is the *Hidden Markov Model*, but neural networks are also used and in some cases, hybrid processes using a combination of these two approaches. The models are tuned through a process of training using large amounts of training data. Usually, hundreds to thousands of audio hours are employed in order to handle the variability and complexity of human speech. The result is an *acoustic model* that represents the different ways in which the sounds and words of a language can be pronounced.

On its own, the acoustic model is not sufficient for high performance speech recognition. An additional part of a speech recognition system is another statistical model, the *language model*. This model contains knowledge about permissible sequences of words and which words are more likely in a given sequence. For example, although acoustically the words *to* and *two* sound the same, the former is more likely in the phrase *I went to the shops* and the latter in the phrase *I bought two shirts*. The language model would help to return the correct word in each phrase.

The output of speech recognition is a list of recognition results (known as the *N-best list*) ranked according to the confidence the recognizer has that the recognition is correct, in an interval from 0 to 1. A value close to 1.0 indicates high confidence that the recognition is correct, while values closer to 0.0 indicate low confidence. The N-best list and the confidence scores are useful as it may be the case that the first-best recognized string is not what the user actually said and that the alternatives might offer a result that is more appropriate. The confidence scores are also useful as they can provide a basis for deciding how the system should continue, for example, whether to confirm the recognized phrase or not.

Using Google speech recognition

Speech recognition services have been available on Android devices since Android 2.1 (API level 7). One place where recognition is available is via a microphone icon on the Android keyboard. Clicking on the microphone button activates the Google speech recognition service, as shown in the following screenshot. The red microphone and the textual prompt indicate that the system is expecting some speech:

If no speech is detected, a re-prompt dialog is generated, asking the user to try to speak again. Another possible situation is where no suitable match can be found for the user's spoken input. In this case, the screen displays the message **No matches found**. Finally, the message **Connection problem** is displayed when no internet connection is available.

The parameters of the on-board speech recognition services can be adjusted either through **Settings | Language and input | Speech | Voice Search** or, depending on the device, by clicking on the **Tool** icon at the top hand corner of the screen. A number of available languages will be presented. Checking for the availability of languages and also selecting a language can be done programmatically. This will be covered in *Chapter 7, Multilingual and Multimodal Dialogs*.

Developing applications with the Google speech recognition API

The components of the Google speech API (package android.speech) are documented at http://developer.android.com/reference/android/speech/package-summary.html. Interfaces and classes are listed here and further details can be obtained by clicking on them.

There are two ways in which speech recognition can be carried out on an Android device: based solely on a RecognizerIntent approach, or by creating an instance of SpeechRecognizer. The former provides an easy-to-program mechanism with which it is possible to create apps that use speech recognition by starting the Intent class and processing its results. The apps following this scheme will present a dialog providing feedback to the user on whether the ASR is ready, or about different errors during the recognition process. Using SpeechRecognizer provides developers with different notifications of recognition-related events, thus allowing a more fine-grained processing of the speech recognition process. With this approach the dialog is not shown, providing more control for the developer on the app's GUI.

In the following sections, we will present two apps (ASRWithIntent and ASRWithLib) that recognize what the user says and present the results for the recognition in the form of an N-best list with confidence scores. In essence, they are the same application but they have been developed following the two different approaches described: ASRWithIntent uses the RecognizerIntent approach, and ASRWithLib the SpeechRecognizer approach which we have programmed in the ASRLib library (sandra.libs.asr.asrlib in the code bundle).

ASRWithIntent app

This simple app illustrates the following:

1. The user selects the parameters for speech recognition.

2. The user presses a button and says some words.

3. The words recognized are displayed in a list along with their confidence scores.

In the opening screen, there is a button with the message **Press the button to speak**. When the user presses the button, speech recognition is launched using the parameters selected by the user. The results of an instance of activating speech recognition and saying the words *What's the weather like in Belfast* are shown in the following screenshot:

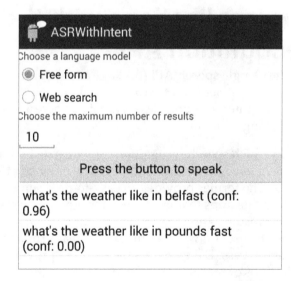

The button that the user presses to start speech recognition is set up through reference to the button specified in `asrwithintent.xml`, which you can find in the code bundle (in the `res/layout` folder of the `ASRWithIntent` project):

```
//Gain reference to speak button
Button speak = (Button) findViewById(R.id.speech_btn);
//Set up click listener
speak.setOnClickListener(
        new View.OnClickListener() {
        @Override
        public void onClick(View v) {
                //Speech recognition does not currently work on simulated
                devices,
                //it is the user attempting to run the app in a simulated
                device
                //they will get a Toast
                if("generic".equals(Build.BRAND. toLowerCase())){
                    Toast toast = Toast.makeText(getApplicationCon
                    text(),"ASR is not supported on virtual devices",
                    Toast.LENGTH_SHORT);
                    toast.show();
                    Log.d(LOGTAG, "ASR attempt on virtual device");
                }
                else{
                    setRecognitionParams(); //Read parameters from GUI
                    listen(); //Set up the recognizer and start listening
                }
        }
    }
});
```

When the user presses the button, the method `listen()` is invoked in which the details of `RecognizerIntent` are set. In `ASRWithIntent`, speech recognition is supported by the class `RecognizerIntent` by sending an Intent with the action `ACTION_RECOGNIZE_SPEECH`, using the method `startActivityForResult(Intent, int)`, where the `int` value is a request code defined by the developer. If it is greater than 0, this code will be returned in `onActivityResult()` when the activity exits. The request code serves as an identifier to distinguish which intent generated a certain result from the different intents that could have been invoked within the application.

The following code starts an activity to recognize speech:

```
Intent intent = new Intent(RecognizerIntent.ACTION_RECOGNIZE_SPEECH);
// Specify language model
intent.putExtra(RecognizerIntent.EXTRA_LANGUAGE_MODEL, languageModel);
// Specify how many results to receive. Results listed in order of
confidence
intent.putExtra(RecognizerIntent.EXTRA_MAX_RESULTS,
numberRecoResults);
// Start listening
startActivityForResult(intent, ASR_CODE);
```

As shown in the code, there are a number of extras associated with
ACTION_RECOGNIZE_SPEECH. One of these, EXTRA_LANGUAGE_MODEL, is required.
The others are optional. As its name implies, EXTRA_LANGUAGE_MODEL specifies the
language model to be used in the recognition process. The following two options
are supported by it:

- LANGUAGE_MODEL_FREE_FORM: This language model is based on free-form
  speech recognition and is used to recognize free-form speech, for example,
  in the dictation of an e-mail.

- LANGUAGE_MODEL_WEB_SEARCH: This language model is based on web search
  terms and is used to model more restricted forms of input such as shorter,
  search-like phrases, for example, *flights to London*, *weather in Madrid*, and
  so on.

As can be observed, both options imply quite unrestricted inputs. To build an app
in which only certain keywords are accepted, or to use recognition grammars,
currently it is necessary to post-process the recognition results to match them against
the expected patterns. Some examples on how to do this will be shown in *Chapter 6,
Grammars for Dialog*.

The other extras are described in the Android documentation for the
RecognizerIntent class. The following are some of the more commonly
used optional extras:

- EXTRA_PROMPT: This provides a text prompt that is shown to users when
  they are asked to speak.

- EXTRA_MAX_RESULTS: This integer value specifies a limit on the maximum
  number of results to be returned. If omitted, the recognizer will choose
  how many results to return. The results are the different possible texts
  corresponding to the user's input and sorted from most to less probable
  (the N-best list discussed earlier in this chapter).

- EXTRA_LANGUAGE: This specifies a language that can be used instead of the default provided on the device. The use of other languages is covered in *Chapter 7, Multilingual and Multimodal Dialogs*.

The user can be asked to choose from these options or they can be set programmatically. The ASRWithIntent app prompts the user for the language model and the maximum number of results. If the information is not provided, it uses the default values indicated in two constants (see the showDefaultValues and setRecognitionParams methods in the asrwithintent.java file).

The results of the speech recognition are returned via activity results in onActivityResults(int, int, Intent). At this point, the recognition is complete. However, normally we would want to see the results or use them in some way. The additional steps required for this are illustrated in the following annotated code from ASRWithIntent:

```
protected void onActivityResult(int requestCode, int resultCode,
Intent data) {
    if (requestCode == ASR_CODE) {
        if (resultCode == RESULT_OK) {
            //Retrieves the N-best list and the confidences from the
            ASR result
            ArrayList<String> nBestList =
                data.getStringArrayListE xtra(RecognizerIntent.EXTRA_
                RESULTS);
            float[] nBestConfidences =
                data.getFloatArrayExtra(RecognizerIntent.EXTRA_
                CONFIDENCE_SCORES;

            /** Creates a collection of strings, each one with a
            recognition result and its confidence, e.g. "Phrase matched
            (conf: 0.5)" */
            ArrayList<String> nBestView = new ArrayList<String>();

            for(int i=0; i<nBestList.size(); i++){
                if(nBestConfidences[i]<0)
                    nBestView.add(nBestList.get(i) + " (no confidence
                    value available)");
                else
                    nBestView.add(nBestList.get(i) + " (conf: " +
                    nBestConfidences[i] + ")");
            }

            //Includes the collection in the listview of the GUI
            setListView(nBestView);
```

```
                    //Adds information to log
                    Log.i(LOGTAG, "There were : "+ nBestView. size()+"
                    recognition results");
            }
            else {
                    //Reports error in log
                    Log.e(LOGTAG, "Recognition was not successful");
            }
        }
    }
```

As discussed earlier, the recognition results are returned through the intent. The matched sentences are accessible using the method `getStringArrayListExtra` using `RecognizerIntent.EXTRA_RESULTS` as a parameter. Similarly, an array with the confidence scores can be obtained with `getFloatArrayExtra` and `RecognizerIntent.EXTRA_CONFIDENCE_SCORES`.

The results are held in a new `ArrayList<String>`, the elements of which combine the strings from the matches and scores (represented as strings) from the float array. Note that there is a possibility that the confidence score is -1; this is the case when the confidence score is unavailable. Then, `ArrayAdapter` is called in the `setListView` method to insert the formatted strings into the `ListView` method of the GUI.

It might also happen that the recognition could not be carried out satisfactorily (`resultCode!=RESULT_OK` in the previous code). There are different constants for the main error situations defined in the `RecognizerIntent` class: RESULT_AUDIO_ERROR, RESULT_CLIENT_ERROR, RESULT_NETWORK_ERROR, RESULT_SERVER_ERROR, and RESULT_NOMATCH. They all correspond to errors due to the physical device or the network, except for the last one that corresponds to the situation in which no phrase matched the audio input. Developers can use the result code to carry out a detailed treatment of these errors. However, the dialog shown already implements a naive treatment of such errors which may suffice for simpler apps. In this case, the user receives feedback on the errors and when it is applicable, they are asked to repeat their utterance.

Finally, since the app needs to access the Internet to carry out speech recognition, it is necessary to set the permission in the `manifest` file:

```
<uses-permission android:name="android.permission.INTERNET" />
```

ASRWithLib app

The ASRWithLib app has exactly the same functionality as ASRWithIntent, but
instead of solely using a RecognizerIntent class, it creates an instance of the
SpeechRecognizer class. In order to make the code usable in all the apps that
employ ASR, we propose to use a library as we did in the previous chapter for
TTS. In this case, the library is in sandra.libs.asr.asrlib and contains only
one class ASR, which implements the RecognitionListener interface, and thus
all the methods that cope with the different recognition events namely onResults,
onError, onBeginningOfSpeech, onBufferReceived, onEndOfSpeech, onEvent,
onPartialResults, onReadyForSpeech, and onRmsChanged.

The SpeechRecognizer instance is created in the createRecognizer method after
checking that the ASR engine is available in the device:

```
List<ResolveInfo> intActivities = packManager.
queryIntentActivities(new Intent(RecognizerIntent.ACTION_RECOGNIZE_
SPEECH), 0);

if (intActivities.size() != 0) {
    myASR = SpeechRecognizer.createSpeechRecognizer(ctx);
    myASR.setRecognitionListener(this);
}
```

This code queries the PackageManager class to check whether recognition is
supported. If the value of intActivities.size() is greater than zero, speech
recognition is supported, and an instance of SpeechRecognizer is then created
and saved in the attribute myASR. The listener for recognition is set using a reference
to this, as the ASR class implements the RecognitionListener interface.

The listen method is used to start listening using a RecognizerIntent class.
Although the extras are the same as in the ASRWithIntent app, the way in
which the recognition is started is slightly different. ASRWithIntent used
startActivityForResult while in this case, the SpeechRecognizer object
is in charge of starting the recognition receiving the intent as an argument.

```
public void listen(String languageModel, int maxResults) throws
Exception{

        if((languageModel.equals(RecognizerIntent.LANGUAGE_MODEL_FREE_
        FORM) || languageModel.equals(RecognizerIntent.LANGUAGE_MODEL_
        WEB_SEARCH)) && (maxResults>=0){
            Intent intent =
                new Intent(RecognizerIntent.ACTION_RECOGNIZE_SPEECH);
            // Specify the calling package to identify the application
```

```
        intent.putExtra(RecognizerIntent.EXTRA_CALLING_PACKAGE, ctx.
        getPackageName());

        // Specify language model  intent.putExtra(RecognizerIntent.
        EXTRA_LANGUAGE_MODEL,
        languageModel);

        // Specify how many results to receive.
        // Results listed in order of confidence
        intent.putExtra(RecognizerIntent.EXTRA_MAX_RESULTS,
        maxResults);

        // Start recognition
        myASR.startListening(intent);
    }
    else
        throw new Exception("Invalid parameters for listen method");
}
```

In the `ASRWithIntent` app, all the code was in the same class and the testing for the correctness of the recognition parameters (`languageModel` and `maxResults`) was carried out in that single class. However, here we are building a library that will be used in many apps, thus it is not possible to take for granted that the parameters will be checked before invoking the `listen` method. This is why the method checks their values and throws an exception if they are not correct.

Several methods are used to react to the different events that can be raised by the ASR engine. It is not a good policy to implement the response to such events in the library, firstly because it would imply that all apps that use the library make the same management of these events; secondly because most of the time responding to the events involves showing messages to the user or using the GUI in some other way, and it is a basic design principle to separate the logic of the application from its interface.

That is why the ASR class employs abstract methods. Abstract methods only declare the header, and it is the responsibility of the subclasses to provide the code for them. This way, each of the methods in charge of responding to ASR events invokes an abstract method, and the behavior of such methods varies for each of the subclasses of ASR. In the `ASRWithLib` example, the `ASRWithLib` class is a subclass of ASR and implements the abstract methods in a certain way. If we had another app in which we wanted to develop a different behavior, we could write separate code for those methods.

For example, the `onResults` method from the `ASR.java` class is invoked when the engine finds sentences that match what the user said. The code for this method in `ASR.java` is as follows. Note that to retrieve the results, it uses static methods from the `SpeechRecognizer` class, and not from `RecognizerIntent` as in `ASRWithIntent`:

```
public void onResults(Bundle results) {
processAsrResults(results.getStringArrayList(SpeechRecognizer.RESULTS_
RECOGNITION),results.getFloatArray(SpeechRecognizer.CONFIDENCE_
SCORES));
}
```

This method invokes the abstract method `processAsrResults`. It is in the `ASRWithLib` class where this method is implemented, indicating how to process the results (in this case by populating a list view as in `ASRWithIntent`).

As you might have observed, the `ASRWithLib` app does not show the recognition dialog. This may be desirable in apps that perform continuous speech recognition (ASR is always active as a background service), for which such feedback can be annoying for the user. However, for other apps it is necessary to show some feedback to the user so that they know that the app is listening. This is carried out with the `onAsrReadyForSpeech` method. This method is executed when the ASR engine is ready to start listening, and is an abstract method from `ASRLib` implemented in `ASRWithLib.java` by changing the color and message of the speech button (both the text and color are not hard-coded but are retrieved from the `res/values` folder):

```
Button button = (Button) findViewById(R.id.speech_btn);
button.setText(getResources().getString(R.string.speechbtn_listening));
button.setBackgroundColor(getResources().getColor(R.color.speechbtn_
listening));
```

Finally, it is necessary to set the permissions in the `manifest` file to access the Internet for using ASR and to record audio:

```
<uses-permission android:name="android.permission.INTERNET" />
<uses-permission android:name="android.permission.RECORD_AUDIO"/>
```

Summary

This chapter has shown how to use the Google speech API to implement speech recognition services, having checked that they are available on the device. The user is prompted to say some words and the results of the recognition, the recognized strings and their confidence scores, are displayed on the screen. The user can choose the language model for recognition and the maximum number of results to be retrieved. This functionality has been implemented following two different approaches in the ASRWithIntent and ASRWithLib apps.

The ASRWithIntent app is a basic easy-to-develop example in which all the code is contained in the same class. ASR is carried out using a RecognizerIntent class and there is an automatically generated dialog that provides feedback on whether the engine is listening or if there was any error.

The ASRWithLib app shows how to modularize and create a library for speech recognition that can be used in many apps. Instead of relying on the RecognizerIntent class only, it uses an instance of the SpeechRecognizer class and implements the RecognitionListener interface using abstract methods, providing a flexible implementation that can respond to a wide range of ASR events.

While these two examples are not particularly useful apps as such, the code presented here can be used virtually unchanged in any apps using speech recognition. Future examples in this book will be built on this code. The next chapter will show how TTS and ASR can be combined to perform simple voice interactions in which the user can ask for information or issue a command to the device.

4
Simple Voice Interactions

Wouldn't it be great if you could just speak to your mobile device to ask it for information or to get it to do something? This chapter looks at simple voice interactions that allow you to do just this. Two tutorial examples will show you how to implement a query to search for information as well as a request to launch one of the apps on your device.

Speech recognition is not perfect, thus it is interesting to implement some mechanisms to choose only the best recognition results. In previous chapters, we studied how to obtain confidence measures. In this chapter, we will cover two new mechanisms: similarity measures to compare the recognized input with what the user said, and confirmations to directly ask the user if the system understood correctly.

By the end of this chapter, you should be able to develop simple voice interactions to request information and carry out commands on your device. You should also be aware of how to use similarity measures and confirm what the user has said.

Voice interactions

As discussed in Chapter 1, *Speech on Android Devices*, Google Voice Actions are simple interactions in which the user speaks a question or a command and the app responds with an action or a verbal response (or a combination of both).

The following are examples of similar interactions with a simple structure and involving a small number of turns:

Example 1

User: BBC News

App: (launches BBC News)

Example 2

App: What is your query?

User: What is the capital of France?

App: (returns web pages about Paris and France)

The interactions are simple in the following ways:

- **Limited dialog management**: The interactions consist of at most two or three turns.

- **Limited spoken language understanding**: The user is restricted to inputs consisting of single words or phrases, such as the name of a website or of an app, or a stretch of text that can be handled by the Google search engine.

VoiceSearch app

This app illustrates the following:

1. When clicking on the **Press the button to speak** option, the user is prompted to say some words.

2. The user speaks some words.

3. VoiceSearch initiates a search query based on the words spoken by the user.

The opening screen has a button asking the user to press and speak. On pressing the button, the next screen displays the Google speech prompt **What is your query?** The results are displayed in a browser window.

In this case, the app uses the two libraries developed previously: TTSLib (see Chapter 2, *Text-to-Speech Synthesis*) and ASRLib (see Chapter 3, *Speech Recognition*). Their jar files are included in the libs folder of the VoiceSearch project. The ASR methods are used to recognize the user input and use it as the search criterion. The TTS is employed to provide spoken feedback to the user about the status of the app.

This app combines the code that was already presented for the TTSWithLib (Chapter 2, *Text-to-Speech Synthesis*) and the ASRWithLib (Chapter 3, *Speech Recognition*) apps. It uses an instance of TTS as in TTSWithLib, and the same methods for ASR in ASRWithDemo. It also provides visual feedback on whether the app is listening to the user or not by changing the color and text of the button.

Once the ASR produces a result, it is used to carry out a Google search using a web search intent, as shown in the processAsrResults method:

```
public void processAsrResults(ArrayList<String> nBestList, float[]
nBestConfidences) {
        String bestResult = nBestList.get(0);
        indicateSearch(bestResult); //Provides feedback to the user that
        search
        //is going to be started
        //Carries out a web search with the words recognized
        Intent intent = new Intent(Intent.ACTION_WEB_SEARCH);
        intent.putExtra(SearchManager.QUERY, bestResult);
        startActivity(intent);
}
```

As can be observed, the app always initiates a web search using the best result. However, the system might have misrecognized what the user said, in which case the search launched would be incorrect. In order to avoid this situation, it is possible to make use of confirmations. An introduction to confirmations and a simple example using the VoiceSearch app will be presented at the end of this chapter.

VoiceLaunch app

The functionality of this app is as follows:

1. When clicking on the **Press to speak** button, the user is prompted for the name of an app.
2. The user says the name of an app.
3. VoiceLaunch compares the recognized input against the names of all the apps installed in the device, and launches the one whose name is the most similar.

An application like VoiceLaunch does not require any interface, as the user could just speak the name of the app they want to be launched. However, for illustration purposes, we have created a simple interface in which the user can choose the values of two parameters: a similarity threshold and a similarity criterion, as shown in the following screenshot. The screenshot shows the scenario in which the user has asked to launch **Email**. VoiceLaunch shows the screen in the figure and launches the **Email** application (the one with the highest similarity, in this case **1.00**):

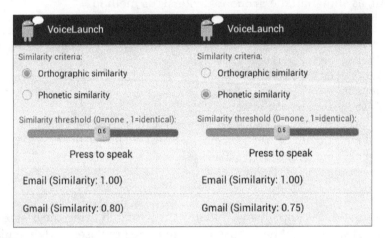

We have introduced the technique of similarity criteria to show how to improve on the results from the ASR. For example, when you have a list of keywords that you want to recognize, but you cannot restrict the ASR to listen only for those words, it is possible that the recognition results are not exactly equivalent to the keywords you expected. For example, if your keywords are ice cream flavors, you may consider *chocolate*, *strawberry*, and *vanilla*, but if your ASR is not restricted, the recognition result for *strawberry* could be *cranberry*. If your app is expecting an exact match, it would discard the recognition result. However with a similarity measure, your app would know that the user said something similar to *strawberry*.

In VoiceLaunch, the similarity criterion is used to control how the app measures the similarity between the name recognized and the names of the apps installed in the device. The similarity threshold is employed so that an app is not launched if its name is not similar enough to what was recognized from the user input.

We consider the following two options for computing similarity:

- **Orthographic similarity**: VoiceLaunch computes Levenshtein distance between the words. This metric considers the distance between words A and B as the minimum number of character insertions, deletions, or substitutions that must be carried out in A to obtain B. VoiceLaunch translates the distance value into a value of similarity between 0 and 1.

- **Phonetic similarity**: `VoiceLaunch` uses the *Soundex* algorithm to compute the phonetic similarity between the names. The implementation used is only valid for English, which is why the `VoiceLaunch` app is only available in this language. In this way, words that sound the same would be considered to be similar even if their spelling is different. The similarity is also measured using the interval from 0 to 1.

> There are many alternatives to the distances considered: Euclidean distance, Jaccard index, Hamming distance, Sorensen similarity index, or Metaphone.

Usually homophones have a similar spelling, so the values for orthographic and phonetic similarity are almost the same, for example, *to* and *too*, or *flower* and *flour*. As can be observed, phonetic similarity is more convenient when working with ASR results, while orthographic similarity is better when working with results from text where misspellings are more frequent. The following table shows some examples:

Similarity criteria	Sample word pairs			
	Addition – Edition	Flower - Flour	Plane – Plain	Browser – Mail
Orthographic similarity	0.75	0.66	0.60	0.00
Phonetic similarity	0.75	1.00	1.00	0.00

> A small Java project to make tests is available on the book's web page. You can make your own tests using the `ComparisonTest` java project. In order to use it, you must include the apache library for Soundex, and include the words to be compared as run parameters. To include the library using Eclipse, right-click on **Project | Properties | Libraries | Add external JARs**. To run the project, right-click on **Run as | Run configurations** and in the **Arguments** tab under **Program arguments**, include the two words separated by a space (for example, `to too`).

The code that deals with the ASR and TTS is similar to the `VoiceSearch` app. However, after the recognition is completed, `VoiceLaunch` must find apps that are similar to the recognized words of the user and launch the one which is the most similar. This is done in the `processAsrResults` method (take a look at it in the code bundle in the `VoiceLaunch.java` file under the `VoiceLaunch` project), which invokes the methods `getSimilarAppsSorted` and `launchApp` that will be described in the following pages.

Have you noticed that...

The use of the ASR library in all the apps enables them to have a similar structure, in which the processing of the recognized information is carried out in the `processAsrResults` method. For example, in the `VoiceSearch` app it started a search with the recognized criteria, while in `VoiceLaunch` it gets the list of similar apps installed and launches the most similar one.

Additionally, `VoiceLaunch` must store and manage information about the apps available on the device. In order to do this efficiently without losing the legibility of the code, we have created an auxiliary class named `MyApp` (you can find it in the code bundle, in `VoiceLaunch.java` under the `VoiceLaunch` project), in which for each app we save its user-friendly name (for example, Adobe Reader), its package name recognizable by Android (for example, com.adobe.reader), and its similarity with the user input (a value from 0 to 1, for example, 0.7).

As it is necessary to sort the installed apps, we also define a comparator for the objects of the `MyApp` class. Comparators return a negative number if the first element is smaller than the second, 0 if they are equal, and a positive number if the first is higher than the second. They can then be employed to sort collections from the minimum to the maximum value. In our case, we want to sort a collection of `MyApps` from the highest to the lowest similarity. Thus, we multiply the results of the comparator of the similarity values by -1 to get the results in the reverse order:

```
private class AppComparator implements Comparator<MyApp>{
    @Override
    public int compare(MyApp app1, MyApp app2) {
        return (- Double.compare(app1.getSimilarity(), app2.
        getSimilarity())); // Multiply by -1 to get reverse ordering
        (from most to least similar)
    }
}
```

As stated before, `VoiceLaunch` uses the method `getSimilarAppsSorted` to obtain the list of apps in the device sorted by similarity, but it only takes into account those apps whose similarity with the recognized name is higher than the specified threshold.

As can be observed in the code bundle (in `VoiceLaunch.java` under the `VoiceLaunch` project), the process is carried out through the following steps:

1. A list of all the installed apps is retrieved from the Package Manager.

2. For each app in the list, its similarity with the recognized name is computed using the algorithm chosen by the user in the GUI. If the similarity value obtained is higher than the threshold, the name, package name, and similarity values for the app are saved by creating an instance of the `MyApp` class, which is added to the `similarApps` collection.

3. The `similarApps` collection is sorted using our similarity comparator:
   `Collections.sort(similarApps, new AppComparator());`

4. The information is saved in the log, so that the developer can be aware of which apps were considered in terms of similarity.

```java
public void processAsrResults(ArrayList<String> nBestList, float[]
nBestConfidences) {

    //Obtains the best recognition result
    String bestResult = nBestList.get(0);

    //Read the values for the similarity parameters from the GUI
    readGUIParameters();
    //Obtains the apps installed in the device sorted from most
    to least similar name regarding the user input

    //String[] = [0] = name, [1] = package, [2] = similarity
    ArrayList<MyApp> sortedApps = getSimilarAppsSorted(bestRes
    ult);

    //Shows the matching apps and their similarity values in a
    list
    showMatchingNames(sortedApps);

    //Launches the best matching app (if there is any)
    if(sortedApps.size()<=0)
    {
        Toast toast = Toast.makeText(getApplicationContex
        t(),"No app found with sufficiently similar name",
        Toast.LENGTH_ SHORT);
        toast.show();
        Log.e(LOGTAG, "No app has a name with similarity >
        "+similarityThreshold);
    }
```

```
        else
            launchApp(sortedApps.get(0));
}
```

You can also try...

An additional method could be used so that the system does not choose one of the similarity measures and selects the most similar app taking into account the results of both the methods, for example, using a weighted voting approach.

Depending on the similarity algorithm employed, `getSimilarAppsSorted` invokes one of the following methods: `compareOrthographic` or `comparePhonetic` (see `VoiceLaunch.java` under the `VoiceLaunch` project in the code bundle). The former computes orthographic distance using the Levenshtein measure, the latter computes the phonetic distance using the Soundex algorithm.

To compute Levenshtein distance, we use the `LevenshteinDistance.java` class in the `com.voicedemos` package. It is based on the code proposed by wikibooks available at `http://en.wikibooks.org/wiki/Algorithm_Implementation/Strings/Levenshtein_distance#Java`, to which we have added the code to translate the distance to a similarity value between 0 and 1.

To compute the phonetic distance, we use the Soundex implementation provided by Apache Commons available at `http://commons.apache.org/proper/commons-codec/index.html`. In order to do this, we have added the `jar` file corresponding to `commons-code-1.8 lib` to the `libs` folder of the `VoiceLaunch` project.

The input parameters of the two similarity calculation methods are two strings, corresponding to the name of the app under consideration and the recognized input. These strings were previously normalized by erasing spaces and using lowercase:

```
private String normalize(String text){
    return text.trim().toLowerCase();
}
```

A more sophisticated normalization could be carried out in order to cope with the situation in which the user says just one word of a two word name, for example, *kindle* instead of *kindle reader*.

Once the apps are ordered, the most similar app is launched using the `launchApp` method, which uses `launchintent` with the package name of the app (you can find it in the `VoiceLaunch.java` file in the code bundle).

VoiceSearchConfirmation app

Confirmations are a very important aspect of a transactional dialog and are also used extensively by humans in service transactions to ensure that everything has been understood correctly. Since the current speech recognition technology cannot guarantee that the app heard exactly what the user said, the app should confirm what the user wants, especially if the next action could result in unrecoverable consequences. However, confirmations should be used judiciously as they prolong the interaction and can be annoying for the user if they are overused.

The `VoiceSearchConfirmation` app has the same functionality as `VoiceSearch`, but it confirms the search criteria before performing the search. Two sample interactions with this app are as follows:

- **Confirmation scenario**: This scenario is characterized by the following steps:
    1. The user pushes the button to talk and says *Weather in Belfast*.
    2. The system understands *Weather in Belfast* and asks *Did you say weather in Belfast?*
    3. The user pushes the button to talk and says *Yes*.
    4. The system launches a search with *Weather in Belfast* as the criterion.

- **Negation scenario**: It is characterized by the following steps:
    1. The user pushes the button to talk and says *Weather in Granada*.
    2. The system understands *Weather in Canada* and asks *Did you say weather in Canada?*
    3. The user pushes the button to talk and says *No*.
    4. The dialogue goes back to step 1 until the user is satisfied.

The `processResults` method is invoked any time the ASR recognizes something from the user input. Thus, in order to provide the app with confirmation capabilities, it is necessary to distinguish whether the method was invoked after recognizing the search criterion or whether it recognized the yes/no response from a confirmation request. In order to do this, we introduce the new attribute `searchCriterion` that stores the criterion recognized. If it is null, we try to recognize a new criterion, if not, we confirm its value. You can take a look at the code in the `VoiceSearchConfirmation.java` file under the `VoiceSearchConfirmation` project of the code bundle.

Other similarity measures and techniques

Other similarity measures and techniques for enhancing the results returned by the Google speech recognizer are described in the book by Greg Milette and Adam Stroud called *Professional Android™ Sensor Programming* in Chapter 17. Among the techniques discussed are:

Using stemming to improve word spotting, that is, reducing words to their roots by removing suffixes, for example, reducing walk, walks, walked, and walking to the same root.

Phonetic indexing, that is, matching words that are similar in terms of how they sound, for example, being able to return *apple* if the recognizer returns the similarly sounding word *appeal*.

Matching using Lucene, a search engine library designed for searching text.

Summary

In this chapter, we have shown how to develop simple voice interactions using the Google speech recognition and TTS APIs. The first example showed how to take an input of some words from the user and initiate a search query. The second example involved using speech to launch apps on the device. Here we introduced the technique of using similarity measures to compare the recognition of the user's input with what might have been said. Two different measures were illustrated: orthographic similarity and phonetic similarity. The final example showed how to use confirmations in order to check with the user that the system had recognized the input correctly. These techniques, along with the use of confidence scores introduced in the previous chapter, are useful tools for the development of speech-enabled apps.

However, these interactions are limited in two ways. Firstly, they do not involve the use of dialog state information to control the interaction and to determine what the app should say and do. The app's behavior is hard-coded within the particular voice action. Secondly, the interactions restrict the user to a simple one word or a short phrase input. More complex dialogs require both a representation of the dialog state and more advanced spoken language understanding. Chapter 5, *Form-filling Dialogs* shows how to include a representation of dialog state in order to provide more flexible dialog management, while Chapter 6, *Grammars for Dialog* shows how to use grammar to allow more advanced spoken language understanding.

As far as confirmations are concerned, we have presented a very naive solution for the case in which only a single piece of data has to be confirmed. In the next chapters, we will study how to create a more sophisticated behavior in which several pieces of data can be confirmed as well as confirmation policies that take into account recognition confidences. We will also introduce an approach that does away with the need to push the button to talk.

5
Form-filling Dialogs

Many speech-enabled apps use one-shot dialogs like the ones described in the previous chapter. Do you feel that speech interfaces can go further than that? Can you imagine more complex interactions in which several items of information have to be elicited from the user for a wide variety of purposes, for example, to launch apps, query databases, start web services or web services mashups, and a lot more?

These types of dialog are similar to form-filling in a traditional web application. By the end of this chapter you should be able to implement simple form-filling dialogs in order to obtain the data necessary to access a web service.

Form-filling dialogs

A form-filling dialog can be seen in terms of a number of slots to be filled. For example, in the case of a flight booking app, the system may have to fill five slots: destination, arrival date, arrival time, departure date, and departure time. In a simple form-filling dialog each slot is processed one at a time and the relevant questions are asked until all the slots have been filled. At that point the app can look up the required flight and present the results to the user. The following is an example of how a dialog might proceed and how status of the slots changes as the dialog progresses.

App: Welcome to the Flight Information Service. Where would you like to travel to?

Caller: London.

Slot	Destination	Arrival date	Arrival time	Departure date	Departure time
Value	London	unknown	unknown	unknown	unknown

App: What date would you like to fly to London?

Caller: The 10th of July.

Slot	Destination	Arrival date	Arrival time	Departure date	Departure time
Value	London	07/10/2013	unknown	unknown	unknown

Frames can also have conditions attached to the slots, for example, if it is a return journey, then values would also be required for the slots of the return leg.

In a more complex dialog the user can fill more than one slot at a time, as in the following example:

App: Welcome to the Flight Information Service. Where would you like to travel to?

Caller: I would like to fly to London on Friday.

Slot	Destination	Arrival date	Arrival time	Departure date	Departure time
Value	London	21/06/2013	unknown	unknown	unknown

As the user has already provided the arrival date in response to the destination question, that slot can be filled and the system can skip the arrival question. However, to process the caller's input in this example more complicated grammars would be required, as discussed in *Chapter 6, Grammars for Dialog*.

Implementing form-filling dialogs

In order to implement form-filling dialogs it is necessary to:

- Create a data structure to represent the slots that will hold the information that the system has to elicit from the user.
- Develop an algorithm to process the slots, extracting the required prompts for each of them.

VoiceXML (http://www.w3.org/TR/voicexml20/) provides a useful structure for this task in terms of forms containing fields that represent the different items of information (slots) required to complete the form. The following code is an example:

```
<form id = "flight">
<field name="destination">
<prompt>where would you like to travel to?</prompt>
<grammar src = "destinations.grxml"/>
</field>
<field name="date">
<prompt>what day would you like to travel?</prompt>
```

```
<grammar src = "days.grxml"/>
</field>
</form>
```

The preceding example shows an app that asks for two pieces of information: destination and date. To ask for destination, it uses the prompt where would you like to travel to?, and to ask for the date it synthesizes what day would you like to travel?. Each piece of data is acquired sequentially by reprompting the user until all the information is collected. In VoiceXML this is done using the **Form Interpretation Algorithm (FIA)** which is further described in http://www.w3.org/TR/voicexml20/#dml2.1.6.

While implementing a complete VoiceXML approach to form-filling is beyond the scope of this book, in the remainder of this chapter we will show how to create a simple form-filling app that makes use of a similar data structure and algorithm.

You can also try...

You can create your own VoiceXML dialogs using **Voxeo Evolution** (http://evolution.voxeo.com/). You can sign up for a free developer account and then you will be able to create your own VoiceXML applications that will be assigned a Skype number that you can use to interact with them. Note that this is not directly useful for Android applications but will provide insight into VoiceXML and how it works as a dialog scripting language.

You might also wish to investigate the use of JVoiceXML (http://jvoicexml.sourceforge.net/) to build a complete VoiceXML parser in Java. The code for an initial implementation for android can be found here: http://sourceforge.net/p/jvoicexml/code/HEAD/tree/branches/android/

Threading

We will use XML files for various purposes in the remaining chapters and have encapsulated the common code in the XMLLib library. One important issue involves threading. When launching an app, a thread is created to run the code. This thread is responsible for the actions that involve updating the user interface, so it is sometimes called the **UI thread**. Carrying out very expensive operations in the UI thread, such as downloading files, carrying out HTTP requests, opening socket connections, or accessing databases, might block the UI thread for a long time, making it unresponsive and freezing updates of the interface. For this reason from Android 3 (HoneyComb) onwards, when trying to perform a networking operation on the main thread of an Android app, the android.os.NetworkOnMainThreadException is raised.

Android provides several ways to enable communication between background threads and the UI thread as explained here: `http://developer.android.com/guide/components/processes-and-threads.html`

One of the alternatives is to use an asynchronous task (`AsyncTask`). The `AsyncTask` runs all the time-consuming operations in the background and publishes the results in the UI thread. The documentation for `AsyncTask` can be found here: `http://developer.android.com/reference/android/os/AsyncTask.html`

In short, when an asynchronous task is executed it undergoes four stages which can be controlled with the methods: `onPreExecute` before the task is executed, `doInBackground` that performs the background computation right after `onPreExecute`, `onProgressUpdate` that displays the progress of the operation (for example, in a progress bar in the user interface), and `onPostExecute`, that is invoked when the background computation is finished.

XMLLib

In our library (`sandra.libs.util.xmllib` in the code bundle), the `RetrieveXMLTask` (see `RetrieveXMLTask.java`) is responsible for fetching an XML file from the web and saving its content in a String to be further processed. It is declared in the following way:

```
class RetrieveXMLTask extends AsyncTask<String, Void, String>
```

It has been defined as an asynchronous task (`AsyncTask`) that receives a collection of Strings as input parameters. It does not produce any type of progress values (void), and produces a String as a result of the background computation (<parameters, progress, result>). In our case, the String input is the URL to retrieve the XML file, and the String result is the XML code in the file. The reading of the XML file from the specified URL is done as a background task in the `doInBackground` method that uses other private methods that open the HTTP connection and read the byte streams (`saveXmlInString` and `readStream`). Take a look at the `doInBackground` and `saveXMLInString` methods in the code bundle (`XMLLib` project, `RetrieveXMLTask.java`). There is a nice tutorial on how to make an asynchronous HTTP request at: `http://mobiledevtuts.com/android/android-http-with-asynctask-example/`

As it can be observed, the management of exceptions in `RetrieveXMLTask` is carried out in a special way, as there is an attribute called `exception` that is used to save the possible exceptions raised during the connection or reading operations (the `doInBackground` method). The management of such exceptions is carried out once the asynchronous task is completed (in the `onPostExecute` method).

Once the background task is finished, we need to provide our results back to the calling class using the `onPostExecute` method. In order to do so, we define the interface `XML AsyncResponse` (see `XML AsyncResponse.java`) with the abstract method `processXMLContents`. The idea is that the class that invokes the asynchronous task implements the interface providing the code for the `processXMLContents` method, and `onPostExecute` delegates the processing of the output to this method (see the `onPostExecute` method in the code bundle: `sandra.libs.util.xmllib.RetrieveXMLTask`).

FormFillLib

To build a form-filling app, we must specify a data structure such as the one in the flight example. To do this, we define two classes: `Form` and `Field`. As shown in the UML diagram, a `Form` has a collection of Fields, and a `Field` has five attributes; a name, a string representing the prompt that the app will use to ask for the piece of data, two strings representing the prompts to be used when the app does not understand the user's response to the initial prompt (`nomatch`), or does not hear it (`noinput`), and the value that has been understood by the app.

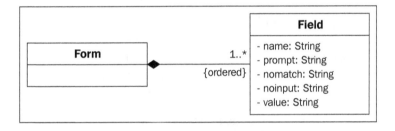

For example, the `Field` flight setting could have the following values for its attributes:

name: Destination

prompt: What is your destination?

nomatch: Sorry, I did not understand what you said

noinput: Sorry, I could not hear you

value: Rome (when the user has said **Rome** in response to the system prompt)

This structure will suffice to build an app of the type we are discussing in this chapter. It is only necessary to create as many objects of the `Field` class as slots to be filled, and a `Form` that contains a collection of the fields in the desired order. This can be easily done programmatically in Java, however it is not very reader-friendly and it is difficult for the programmer to change some parameters like the system prompts.

To solve this, we will implement a subset of the VoiceXML standard to create easy-to-read XML files containing the structure of the dialog. Then, we will use the VXMLParser class to automatically parse the XML files and translate them into objects for the Field and Form classes. Finally, a DialogInterpretation class will use these objects to manage the interaction.

 This does not make the VoiceXML design completely independent from the app. The apps need to know which pieces of information it is necessary to process and these are indicated as fields in the VoiceXML file. Thus, the developer can change anything in the VoiceXML except for the number and name of the fields.

VXMLParser

There are different ways to implement parsers in Android, mainly using DOM, SAX, or a Pull parser. Android recommends the use of the XMLPullParser class (http://developer.android.com/reference/org/xmlpull/v1/XmlPullParser.html), as it has been designed for better performance and simplicity. XML pull parsing allows streaming parsing, where the process can be interrupted and resumed at any time.

In order to parse VXML files, we create an XMLPullParser to read the XML contents, and repeatedly invoke the method next() to retrieve the next event, until the event is END_DOCUMENT. This way, we process the START_TAG, TEXT, and END_TAG events to respectively manage the situations in which the system encounters a starting tag, processes the text inside a tag, or encounters a closing tag.

We create a new Form object when the system encounters the <form> tag. As the idea of the parser is to process a single form, if there were several forms in the file, we would only keep track of the last one. This is done by keeping only one instance of the Form class as an attribute of the VXMLParser class.

With respect to fields, their names are extracted by parsing the attributes of the <field> tag. Then, we also save the information about the prompt, nomatch, and noinput prompts when their corresponding VoiceXML tags are encountered.

Any class using the VoiceXML parser can invoke the parseVXML method (see sandra.libs.dm.fomfilllib.VXMLParser) to obtain the form created when parsing the data. The parser employs the FormFillLibException class in order to carry out a more fine-grained control of exceptions.

DialogInterpreter

The DialogInterpreter resembles the FIA algorithm in VoiceXML. It visits all the fields in sequential order until the app obtains a speech recognition result for each of them. In each field, it synthesizes the prompt and listens for the user input. If speech recognition is successful, then it moves to the next field, if not, the system repeats the process for the current field. The following pseudo code describes the interpreter behavior:

```
Interpret field i:
        Play prompt of field i
        Listen for ASR result
        Process ASR result:
            If the recognition was successful, then save recognized
            keyword as value for the field i and move to the next
            field
            If there was a no match or no input, then interpret field i
            If there is any other error, then stop interpreting

Move to the next field:
        If the next field has already a value assigned, then move to
        the next one
        If the last field in the form is reached, then
        endOfDialogue=true
```

The behavior described in the pseudo code is developed in the DialogInterpreter class. This class uses different attributes to control the interpretation: the Form that must be interpreted, an integer currentPosition that represents the position of the field that must be interpreted in the list of the form's fields, two strings with prompts for the nomatch and noinput events (that will be replaced by the ones parsed from the VoiceXML file if there are any available), and a HashMap that contains the results of the interpretation in the form of pairs of strings <field name, field value>.

Interpretation starts when the startInterpreting method is invoked. The form to be interpreted is provided, the currentPosition is initialized to 0 and the interpretCurrentField is invoked. The interpretCurrentField method does not encapsulate all the behavior shown in the pseudocode for interpret field i, as it is necessary to use different methods to control the various ASR events. Thus, interpretCurrentField only controls the first part: it plays the field prompt and starts ASR. Then, the methods processAsrResults and processAsrErrors from ASRLib are used to account for the different events. The former controls the case in which the ASR understands something from the user's input, saves its value in the Hashmap of results and invokes the moveToNextField method.

The latter controls the case in which there is an error in ASR, if the error code is ERROR_NO_MATCH or ERROR_SPEECH_TIMEOUT (nomatch or noinput), the corresponding prompts are synthetized and the field is interpreted again. If the error is due to network problems, the interpretation is stopped. You can take a look at this method in the code bundle (sandra.libs.dm.formfilllib.DialogInterpreter).

The moveToNextField method is similar to the pseudocode shown earlier: it moves the position of the current field forward while the field does not have a value. If there is a field without a value, it is interpreted, if there are no more fields to interpret, the interpretation is finished and the processDialogResults method is invoked.

The processDialogResults method is abstract so that any subclass of DialogInterpreter can provide its own code to process the results of the interpretation. In the next section, we will show an app that uses the FormFillLib library and implements this method to use the results of the dialog to invoke a web service.

You can also try...

Another interesting alternative is to code the structure of the dialog in different data structures in the Java code. This is the approach followed in the *Pizza Ordering App* example (Chapter 15) from Deitel, P., Deitel, H., Deitel, A. and Morgano, M., *Android for Programmers: An App-Driven Approach*, Prentice Hall 2011, which you can find here: http://ptgmedia.pearsoncmg.com/imprint_downloads/informit/bookreg/9780132121361/android_15_speech_final_a.pdf.

The advantage of the approach that we are using is that we provide different libraries to parse and manage the interaction, which are reusable by any app that requires an interface with a basic form-filling dialog. Thus, it is a general purpose approach in which the details for each particular app are supplied in a simple VoiceXML file. An example is shown in the next section.

MusicBrain app

To illustrate how to use the `FormFillLib` we will develop an app that asks the user for the pieces of data necessary to query a web service. The relations between the classes in the app and the libraries described in this chapter are shown in the following class diagram:

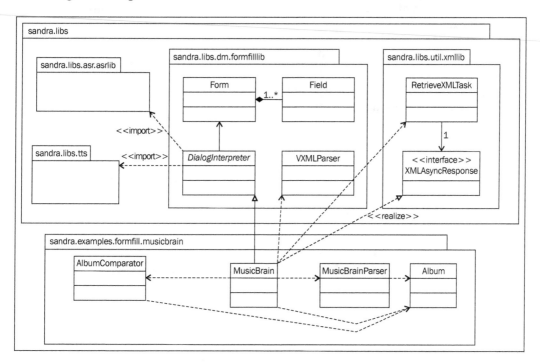

Apps are no longer standalone isolated applications; usually they combine their own resources with data and functionalities gathered from third-party web services. Recently, many web applications have published APIs (Application Programming Interfaces) that allow interested developers to use them in their own apps. This integration can be as complex as desired, involving multiple sources. These are known as mashups. For example, a travel mashup can integrate Google maps to indicate geographical locations with Flickr to show pictures of the relevant tourist attractions while at the same time checking for good restaurants in FoodSpotting.

A list of a wide range of available APIs can be found at: http://www. programmableweb.com. Some of these (for example, Amazon, Google, and Facebook) require you to register in order to use their APIs. Others can only be used by licensed partners, and some are open and available for public (usually non-profit) use.

For the `MusicBrain` app (`sandra.examples.formfill.musicbrain`) we will use the **MusicBrainZ** public API. MusicBrainZ (`http://musicbrainz.org/`) is an open music encyclopedia that contains metadata for music. It allows the user to query about areas (music from a certain place), artists or groups, albums, and releases.

The MusicBrain app provides information about albums released between two dates whose title contains a certain text. A sample interaction with the app is the following excerpt:

App> **Please say a word of the album title**

User> robot

App> **Please say a starting date for the search**

User > 1970

App> **Please say a final date for the search**

User> 2000

The result of the preceding interaction produces the result as shown in the following screenshot:

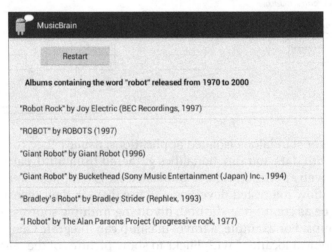

The form-filling dialog is started when the activity is created in `MusicBrain.java`. This involves retrieving the VoiceXML file, parsing it, and interpreting it to obtain the three pieces of data (word in title, starting year and final year) that will be used to query the MusicBrainZ web service. The VoiceXML code is as follows:

```
<form>
<field name="query">
<prompt>Please say a word in the album title</prompt>
```

```
<noinput> Sorry, I could not hear you </noinput>
<nomatch> Sorry, I did not understand what you said </nomatch>
</field>
<field name="initialyear">
<prompt>Please say the starting year for the search</prompt>
<noinput> Sorry, I could not hear you </noinput>
<nomatch> Sorry, I did not understand what you said </nomatch>
</field>
<field name="finalyear">
<prompt>Please say the final year for the search</prompt>
<noinput> Sorry, I could not hear you </noinput>
<nomatch> Sorry, I did not understand what you said
</nomatch>
</field>
</form>
```

Once the dialog is over, the app queries MusicBrainZ and obtains an XML with all the albums whose titles contain the word uttered by the user, then the XML is parsed and filtered to keep just the albums released between the dates selected. Finally the information is shown to the user in the GUI.

 Web services usually provide the results in XML or JSON. We have used the XML version of MusicBrainZ because it is more stable in this particular API, though you might be interested in considering other options when using other web services.

The speech dialog is controlled with the startDialog, processXMLContents, and processDialogResults methods. The startDialog method initializes the ASR and TTS engines (using the ASRLib and TTSLib libraries described in the previous chapters) and starts retrieving the VoiceXML file. As explained earlier, when the VoiceXML file is retrieved, the processXMLContents method is invoked. As there are two possible XML files being retrieved in the app (the VoiceXML with the dialog, and the XML with the results from the web service), the processXMLContents method checks what is the current XML being processed and starts the corresponding parsing procedure. Finally, the processDialogResults method is invoked when the VoiceXML parsing is finished. This method queries MusicBrainZ using the word inside the album title uttered by the user during the dialog. Take a look at the startDialog and processDialogResult methods in the code bundle (MusicBrain. java, MusicBrain project).

The results of the query to the web service are coded in an XML file with the structure explained in `http://musicbrainz.org/doc/Development/XML_Web_Service/ Version_2/Search#Release`. This file is parsed in the method `parseMusicResults`. This method makes use of the `MusicBrainParser` class (see `MusicBrainParser.java`) in which we have implemented an `XMLPullParser`. The parser iterates through the XML file obtaining a collection of albums. To do so, we have defined the `Album` class, which contains information about each album title, interpreter, release date, country, and label.

We use alert dialogs to show the reasons for parsing, ASR, or TTS errors. This way, the user will be better aware of the fact that the app is not working because of ill-formed XMLs or Internet connection problems. The method used to create them is `createAlert` (in `MusicBrain.java`).

Once the XML file has been parsed into a collection of `Album` objects, these are filtered using the `filterAlbums` method (`MusicBrain.java`). This way, from all the albums whose title contains the desired word, we only take into account those that were released between the dates provided by the user. If the recognition results cannot be parsed as dates, then all albums are considered.

Once the albums have been filtered, we show them on the GUI with the method `showResults`. It is not necessary to sort the albums a posteriori, as we have saved them in a `TreeSet`, a collection that allows us to avoid duplicates and to save its elements in order. To do so, we override the `equals` method in `Album.java` using code to compare if two albums are equal (we check whether they have the same title and interpreter), and we create a custom comparator in `AlbumComparator.java` that compares the albums according to their release date so that they can be sorted from the most to the least recent.

Summary

This chapter has shown how to implement form-filling dialogs in which the app engages in simple conversations with the user in order to retrieve several pieces of data which can later be used to provide advanced functionalities to the user through web services or mashups.

The `FormFillLib` contains the classes to retrieve and parse an XML definition of the dialog structure into Java objects. These objects are employed to control the oral interaction with the user. This library makes it possible to easily build any form-filling dialog in an Android app by specifying its structure in a simplified VoiceXML file accessible on the Internet.

The `MusicBrain` app shows how to use the library to gather information from the user through a spoken conversation to query a web service. In this case, the app asks the user for a word and two dates which are used to query the MusicBrainZ open music encyclopedia for albums with the word in their title and those released between the specified dates. The example also shows how to parse and filter the results provided by the web service so that they can be presented to the user.

In this example the ASR input is not restricted, but in many applications it is desirable to limit the vocabulary or phrases that the user might employ. In *Chapter 6, Grammars for Dialog*, we will study how to use grammars that impose some limits on the input while at the same time allowing quite complex structures as well as adding semantics to provide an interpretation of the input.

6
Grammars for Dialog

You will have noticed that the inputs in the form-filling dialogs studied in the previous chapter were restricted to single words and phrases. This chapter introduces the use of grammars to interpret more complex inputs and also to extract their meaning. Two types of grammars in common use for commercial applications are hand-crafted grammars for input that is predictable and well-defined, and statistical grammars for more robust performance with the less well-formed input typical of conversational speech.

By the end of this chapter, you should be able to develop apps that support more extended user input, making use of hand-crafted as well as statistical grammars.

Grammars for speech recognition and natural language understanding

Grammars can be used for two different purposes in speech-based apps that are as follows:

- **Speech recognition**: In this case, grammars (also known as language models) specify the words and phrases that the recognizer can expect. For example, if the system is dealing with cities, it should not try to recognize numbers. Speech recognition grammars, as defined by W3C available at `http://www.w3.org/TR/speech-grammar/`, can either be specified explicitly by the developer (hand-crafted grammars) or can be computed from language data (statistical grammars). Speech recognition grammars help to make speech recognition more accurate.

- **Natural language understanding**: The idea is to take the output of the recognizer and assign a semantic interpretation (or meaning) to the words. This can be done in several ways. One method involves determining the structure of the sentence (syntactic analysis) and then assigning a semantic interpretation (or meaning) to this structure. Alternatively, the semantic interpretation may be extracted directly from the sentence without going through the syntactic analysis stage.

Currently, the Google speech recognition API does not support the use of grammars specified by the developer for speech recognition and the only possible language models are LANGUAGE_MODEL_FREE_FORM and LANGUAGE_MODEL_WEB_SEARCH, which are built into the API. In the applications to be presented in this chapter, we will carry out speech recognition as in the previous chapters and then filter the recognition results and keep only those results that conform to the grammar and use them to obtain a semantic interpretation of the user's input.

You may also try...

Although it is currently not possible to use grammars within Android's RecognizerIntent, it is possible to use third-party options. Visit our web page for further details.

NLU with hand-crafted grammars

Designing a grammar involves predicting the different things the user might say and creating rules to cover them. Grammar design is an iterative process of creating an initial grammar, collecting data to test the grammar against actual user input, adding some phrases and removing others, and so on until the coverage of the grammar is as complete as possible. There are various tools to help with the design of grammars. For example, Nuance provides the Nuance Grammar Builder which can be used to test the coverage of a grammar, to check that the test phrases receive the correct semantic interpretation, and to test for over-generation that is, detect any unnecessary or unexpected phrases in the input (http://evolution.voxeo.com/library/grammar/grammar-gsl.pdf).

There are different languages for specifying speech grammars, the most popular are XML and **Augmented BNF (ABNF)**, defined by W3C available at http://www.w3.org/TR/speech-grammar/, **Java Script Grammar Format (JSGF)** which is used by the Java Speech API, and **Grammar Specification Language (GSL)**, a format that is proprietary to Nuance.

In this chapter, we will use the XML format and present a library that is able to parse simple XML grammars for their use in form-filling dialog like the ones studied in the previous chapter. Developing a full XML grammar processor is beyond the scope of this book, but additional information about the functionalities that it should have can be found in the W3C Speech Recognition Grammar Specification available at `http://www.w3.org/TR/speech-grammar/#S5`.

The following is a simple grammar using some of the tags from the XML grammar format. This grammar can recognize the sentence *show flights to London*:

```
<grammar root = "flight_query">

<rule id = "flight_query">
    <item>show</item>
    <item>flights</item>
    <ruleref uri = "destination" />
</rule>

<rule id = "destination">
    <item> to London </item>
</rule>

</grammar>
```

As can be seen, the grammar is structured in terms of rules. The `<grammar>` tag indicates the starting element (or root) of the grammar which is labeled as `flight_query`. The first rule after the `<grammar>` tag must have the same name as the root element. This rule consists of two items: the word `show` and the word `flights`, which cover the first two words of the string to be processed. The third part is a reference `<ruleref>` to another rule called `destination`. This rule contains the words `to London`. Thus by applying all the rules staring at the root, we can process the string *show flights to London*.

The rule reference is useful when there might be several alternatives; in this case, several alternative destinations. The `<one-of>` tag allows the specification of alternative items. So, for example, we could expand the destination rule as follows:

```
<rule id = "destination">
    <one-of>
            <item> to London </item>
            <item> to Paris </item>
            <item> to New York </item>
    </one-of>
</rule>
```

Indeed, as the word *to* is common to all the phrases in this rule, we could create a further rule reference to city words, as shown in the following more extensive grammar. In this way, a complex hierarchy of rules can be created to specify a wide range of possible input.

Sometimes, words or phrases may be optional or they may be repeated more than once. The repeat attribute allows the use of repetitions using the following specifications, in which n and m are natural numbers:

```
<item repeat="n">        The item repeats n times
<item repeat="n-m">      The item repeats from n to m times
<item repeat="m-">       The item repeats at least m times
```

For example, for a five digit postal code, the item should be as follows:

```
<item repeat="5"><one-of><item>0</item><item>1</item> …<item>9</item></one-of></item>
```

<item repeat="0-1"> indicates that a certain item is optional. In the following grammar, the flight_query, flights, and time rules specify optional elements. This means that a valid input requires only origin, destination, and depart_day and the other information is optional.

Given a combination of the various tags and attributes, we can create a grammar to allow inputs such as the following:

- I would like a flight from Paris to New York on Monday morning
- Show me flights from London to Paris on Tuesday
- From New York to London on Monday afternoon
- From Paris to London on Wednesday

The following is a grammar that can be used to process these and a wide range of other alternative inputs:

```
<grammar root="flight_query">

<rule id="flight_query">
    <ruleref uri="verb"/>
    <ruleref uri="flights"/>
    <ruleref uri="origin"/>
    <ruleref uri="destination"/>
    <ruleref uri="depart_day"/>
    <ruleref uri="depart_time"/>
</rule>
```

```
<rule id="verb">
    <item repeat="0-1">
      <one-of>
            <item><tag>show</tag>Show me</item>
            <item><tag>show</tag>I would like</item>
            <item><tag>show</tag>Are there any</item>
      </one-of>
    </item>
</rule>

<rule id="flights">
    <item repeat="0-1">
        <one-of>
            <item><tag>1</tag>a flight</item>
            <item><tag>N</tag>flights</item>
        </one-of>
    </item>
</rule>

<rule id="origin"> <item>from</item> <ruleref uri="city"/> </rule>
<rule id="destination"> <item>to</item> <ruleref uri="city"/> </rule>
<rule id="depart_day"> <item>on</item> <ruleref uri="day"/> </rule>
<rule id="depart_time"> <ruleref uri="time"/> </rule>

<rule id="city">
    <one-of>
        <item><tag>LHR</tag>London</item>
        <item><tag>CDG</tag>Paris</item>
        <item><tag>JFK</tag>New York</item>
    </one-of>
</rule>

<rule id="day">
    <one-of>
        <item><tag>M</tag>Monday</item>
        <item><tag>T</tag>Tuesday</item>
        <item><tag>W</tag>Wednesday</item>
    </one-of>
</rule>

<rule id="time">
    <item repeat="0-1">
        <one-of>
            <item><tag>a.m.</tag>morning</item>
```

```
                    <item><tag>p.m</tag>afternoon</item>
               </one-of>
          </item>
     </rule>

</grammar>
```

`<tag>` is used to return a value for an item that is different from the words recognized in the input. This is useful for dealing with synonyms where words with the same meaning should return a single value instead of the literal words recognized, or to return a value that is more useful in other components of the app. The following is a simple example:

```
<item><tag>M</tag>Monday</item>
```

Here, if the word `Monday` is processed, the value `M` is returned.

More generally, an app may not need a complete transcription of the input to be able to carry out further processing of what the user said, as it could be enough and even more efficient to use some intermediate (semantic) representation using the `<tag>` tag. Usually, semantic interpretation tags follow the W3C format presented in `www.w3.org/TR/semantic-interpretation/`, which is parsed and processed as ECMAScript objects. This means that it is possible to include small excerpts of code within semantic tags.

In this chapter, we will carry out a very simple treatment of semantics by specifying plain text tags. For example, in the previous grammar we have included tags that specify the code for the main airport of each city so that the semantic interpretation for `destination` is *CDG* (the code for Charles de Gaulle airport) when the sentence contains *to Paris*, and that for `departure_time` is *p.m* if the user says *in the afternoon*.

Statistical NLU

Hand-crafted grammars are time consuming to develop and prone to errors. Considerable linguistic and engineering expertise is required to develop a grammar with good coverage and optimized performance. Moreover, the rules of a hand-crafted grammar cannot easily cope with the irregular input that is characteristic of spontaneous spoken language. For example, given the recognized words *I would like a um flight from Paris to New York on Monday no Tuesday afternoon*, our grammar would fail since *um* and *no* are not specified in the rules.

A statistical grammar is an alternative to a hand-crafted grammar. Statistical grammars are learned from data and involve collecting and annotating large amounts of relevant language data. Statistical grammars can cope with irregular input as they do not have to match the input exactly but rather assign probabilities indicating the extent to which a structure or a semantic interpretation matches the input. There are different types of statistical grammar. For the purposes of this chapter, we are interested in a grammar that returns a semantic interpretation as its result given either the input of a text string or the results from the speech recognition component.

One of the disadvantages of statistical grammars is that they require a large amount of training data. While corpora of language data have been collected for a wide variety of real-world applications, these are not publicly available and the costs of purchasing them would be prohibitive for individual developers. Even if the data were available, considerable effort would be required to annotate and train the grammar. Currently there are few APIs available for statistical semantic grammars but one possibility is a web service provided by **Maluuba** (www.maluuba.com), a company that has developed a personal assistant of the same name for Android devices as well as an API for its statistical semantic grammars.

The Maluuba API (known as nAPI) extracts three types of information from an input that are as follows:

- **Category**: It signifies the main topic of the sentence, for example, weather, travel, entertainment, and navigation. Currently, there are 22 categories covered under it.

- **Action**: It explains a specific action or intent to be accomplished within the category, for example, weather has actions such as WEATHER_STATUS for checking the weather and WEATHER_DETAILS for detailed weather information such as wind speed and humidity.

- **Entities**: It gives a key piece of information that has to be extracted, for example, location, dateRange, and time.

The result is returned as a structured object. The following is an example:

User input: what's the weather in Belfast for tomorrow

Maluuba: {"entities":{"dateRange":[{"start":"2013-05-09","end":"2013-05-10"}],"location":["belfast"]},"action":"WEATHER_STATUS","category":"WEATHER"}

Note that in addition to identifying categories, actions, and entities, the grammar also resolves relative references such as *tomorrow* (this example was submitted on 8 May, 2013). Also, the input does not have to be fully grammatical as long as entities can be identified from the input. So, a sentence such as *Weather Belfast tomorrow* would return the same result.

NLULib

We have implemented a library for natural language understanding that contains classes and methods to process hand-crafted and statistical grammars. We have created the NLU class (NLU.java) to encapsulate both, but they could be processed in isolation.

Processing XML grammars

HandCraftedGrammar.java contains the methods for parsing an XML speech grammar, checking whether a phrase is valid in the grammar, and obtaining its semantic representation. We consider a subset of the tags in the XML format, concretely:

Tag	Description	Possible subtags	Possible attributes (attributes marked with * are mandatory)
<grammar>	Specifies the highest level container	<rule>	root*
<rule>	Specifies valid sequences and structures of words and phrases	<one-of> <item> <ruleref>	id*
<one-of>	Specifies a set of alternatives	<one-of> <item> <ruleref>	
<item>	Specifies valid sequences Contains the literals and semantic tags	<tag> <one-of> <item> <ruleref>	repeat
<tag>	Specifies semantic information in the form of a literal		
<ruleref>	Specifies a reference to another rule		uri*

The constructor parses the XML into java objects (see the parse method in the code bundle in sandra.libs.nlu.nlulib.HandCraftedGrammar) and translates the grammar into a regular java expression (see computeRegularExpression in sandra.libs.nlu.nlulib.HandCraftedGrammar in the code bundle).

The parse method uses XmlPullParser to read the XML code into objects, in a similar fashion to the VXML parser developed in the previous chapter, but using arrays to keep track of the nested items, as in this case we can have identical tags nested (for example, see the previously mentioned example of flights wherein several <item> tags are included within another <item> tag).

In this case, we have created the classes `Alternative`, `Item`, `Rule`, `Repeat`, and `RuleReference` to save the results of parsing `one-of`, `item without a repeat argument`, `rule`, `item with repeat argument`, and `rule-ref` tags respectively. The `GrammarElement` class has been defined as a superclass for the rest, so that when a certain class has a collection of any of the other elements, it can use the `GrammarElement` class as a wildcard. For example, the `Alternative` class contains a collection of `GrammarElement` that represents the different alternatives available.

The result of the parsing is a collection of `Rule` objects, which is saved as an attribute of the `HandCraftedGrammar` class. The rules are saved in a `HashMap` in which the keys are their IDs. For example, the structure resulting from parsing the flights rule in the example grammar is represented in the following figure. Note that in order to simplify the generation of regular expressions that facilitate semantic parsing, we do not process the grammar on the fly during recognition but instead parse it into Java objects before the recognition starts:

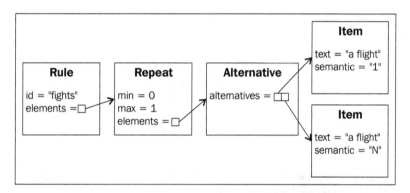

At this point, the `HandCraftedGrammar` constructor has parsed the XML grammar into Java objects with the `parse` method. Then, it uses the objects to compute a regular expression that represents the grammar using the `computeRegularExpression` method. Regular expressions are another way of representing the same information, but they have the advantage that we can directly match the sentences introduced by the user with the grammar using the `Pattern` and `Matcher` classes from the `java.util.regex` API (a tutorial of this API can be found at `http://docs.oracle.com/javase/tutorial/essential/regex/`).

The use of Java objects as a middle step between the XML and the regular expression makes it easier to process the high amount of nested elements and rule references, and allows to generate the regular expression in a bottom-up procedure, starting from the simplest items to the most complex rules.

The computeRegularExpression method (see the code bundle) obtains the regular expression corresponding to the root rule and all the rules to which it makes reference using the getRegExpr() method for each element. This method transforms the information contained in GrammarElement into the regular expression syntax. For example, the translation of the structure in the previous figure is ((a flight) | (flights)) {0, 1}.

The case of RuleReference objects is special because they are translated using the wildcard "xxREFurixx", where uri is the name of the rule being referred to. For example, the depart_day rule is translated as xxREFtimexx.

The solveReferences method in the HandCraftedGrammar class is used to resolve all the references. To do so, the regular expression for the whole grammar is obtained by gradually resolving the references starting from the root. The result for the complete grammar is as follows:

```
(((Show me)|(I would like)|(Are there any)){0,1})(((a
flight)|(flights)){0,1})(from ((London)|(Paris)|(New York)))(to
((London)|(Paris)|(New York)))(on ((Monday)|(Tuesday)|(Wednesday)))
((((morning)|(afternoon)){0,1}))
```

This method also keeps track of the semantic tags. Initially, they are assigned to their corresponding items, for example, the semantic representation JFK is assigned to its item. However, they must be assigned to their corresponding rule in order to be interpretable (that is, to city and then to destination). In order to do so, we use the SemanticParsing class that allows linking tags to rules.

As the regular expression will be the only mechanism used to check the validity of the incoming phrases and loses the structure of the rules, the SemanticParsing class has a position attribute that allows us to determine the group of the regular expression that should match the text that triggers a tag.

Java regular expressions enable the different subclasses of GrammarElement to obtain partial matching results of elements grouped by parentheses, for example, in the previous regular expression the whole matched sentence is in position 0, (((Show me)|(I would like)|(Are there any)){0,1}) is in position 1, ((Show me)|(I would like)|(Are there any)) is in position 2, (Show me) is in position 3, (Are there any) is in position 5, and (on ((Monday)|(Tuesday)|(Wednesday))) is in position 20.

What we do with the SemanticParsing objects is to match the semantic tags with each of these groups. This way, the SemanticParsing object for the depart_time rule indicates that the matching group is in position 20, and that the semantic is M if the expression is on Monday, similarly T for on Tuesday, and W for on Wednesday.

Thus, the semantic representation for the sentence *Show me flights from Paris to New York on Tuesday morning* is as follows:

```
Verb: Show
Flights: N
Origin: CDG
Destination: JFK
Depart_day: T
Depart_time: a.m.
```

The `obtainSemantics` method (see `HandCraftedGrammar.java` in the code bundle) is used to check whether an input matches the grammar, and if it does, what its semantic representation is. This method raises an exception if the grammar is not initialized, that is, if the regular expression of the grammar has not been computed yet (for example, if there was any problem in the constructor with the format of the grammar).

To validate an incoming phrase, we use a Java matcher that automatically checks whether the phrase is compatible with the regular expression. To do so, we ignore whitespaces and use lowercases, as observed in the following piece of code:

```
Pattern p = Pattern.compile(grammarRegExpression.replaceAll("\\s","").
toLowerCase());
Matcher m = p.matcher(utterance.replaceAll("\\s","").toLowerCase());
```

Then, we use the `groupCount` and `group` attribute of the `Matcher` Java class in order to get the phrases that match each of the groups in the regular expression, where a group is each of the patterns between parentheses. This information is then compared with the semantic information and the expected positions saved in the `SemanticParsing` objects, and the semantic representation is saved in a string that is the output of the `obtainSemantics` method.

Processing statistical grammars

To use Maluuba, you need to sign up for a developer's account. Go to Maluuba's developer's website (`http://dev.maluuba.com/`), and click on the tab **Sign up now and receive API access immediately**. Sign up is associated with a Google, Facebook, or GitHub account. Complete the form and then you will be directed to a page where you can create an app. Click on **Create an app** and you will be asked for an **App name** and **App description**. For current purposes, enter something simple, for example, `flights` for **App name** and some text for the description, and you will be given an API key. You can now use this key to send natural language queries to Maluuba, either through your browser or from an Android app. Test the access to the API through your browser as follows:

```
http://napi.maluuba.com/v0/interpret?phase=I would like a flight from
belfast to london on Monday&apikey= <your apikey>
```

`NLU.java` sends a string to Maluuba to obtain a semantic interpretation. You can change the `KEY` attribute to use your developer key. To access the grammar, it uses `XMLLib` described in the previous chapter, so that the URL is accessed safely by means of an asynchronous task.

The result is passed to the invoking method as a string. For example, for the phrase *I would like to go to London*, it returns the following values:

```
{"entities":"destination":["London"]},"action":"NAVIGATION_DIRECTIONS"
,"category":"NAVIGATION"}
```

The GrammarTest app

The `GrammarTest` app (`sandra.examples.nlu.grammartest`) illustrates how to use `NLULib`. It has a simple GUI in which the user selects the type of grammar to be used (hand-crafted or statistical), and can also select the **Check text** or **Check ASR** button to obtain a semantic representation of the input.

In the case of **Check text**, the input is typed into a `TextView` box using the keyboard. In the case of **Check ASR**, the app recognizes an oral input and produces the result for a 10-best list.

In the case of handcrafted grammar, an XML grammar is read from the specified location. The default grammar used is the one presented previously. If the input (either the input text or each of the N-best results) is in the grammar, it shows a valid message and the semantic representation, if not, it shows an invalid message (these messages are not hard-coded, but retrieved from the `Strings` file).

In the case of statistical grammar, the Maluuba service is used. In this case, we do not pose any restrictions on the inputs, so all phrases are considered valid, and a semantic interpretation is shown for each of them.

This app is useful for developers who wish to become familiar with the grammar design process. The following figure shows two screenshots of the app using a handcrafted (left) and a statistical (right) grammar:

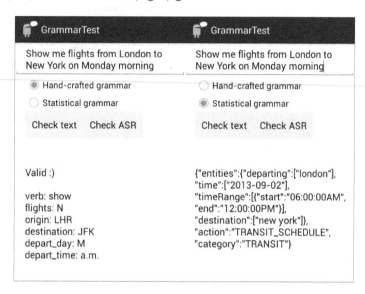

Summary

This chapter has shown how to create and use grammars to check whether the user's input conforms to the words and phrases required by the app. Grammars are also used to extract a semantic representation from the user's input in terms of concepts relevant for the app. Two types of grammar were presented: a hand-crafted grammar designed by the developer to match the requirements of the app, and a statistical grammar learned from a large corpus of relevant data. Hand-crafted grammars are useful for input that is predictable and well-defined, whereas statistical grammars provide more robust performance and can handle a wider range of input that may be less well-formed.

In the chapters so far, the examples have assumed that the language used is English and that the interface is speech-only. *Chapter 7, Multilingual and Multimodal Dialogs*, will look at how to build apps that make use of languages other than English and other modalities in addition to speech.

7
Multilingual and Multimodal Dialogs

In all of the examples so far, the language used has been English and the mode of interaction has been mainly speech. This chapter shows how to incorporate other languages into apps. The chapter also looks at how to build apps that make use of several modalities, for example, combining speech with visual displays.

Multilinguality

In *Chapter 2, Text-to-Speech Synthesis* and *Chapter 3, Speech Recognition*, we have provided the groundwork to enable you to develop multilingual applications easily. With the TTSLib library (*Chapter 2, Text-to-Speech Synthesis*) you can specify the language used for speech synthesis. Now we only need to make some small improvements to the ASRLib (*Chapter 3, Speech Recognition*) to make it accept different languages for speech recognition (as it was set originally to the device's default). To do this, we have created the ASRMultilingualLib (in sandra.libs.asr. asrmultilinguallib) in the code bundle).

We cannot expect that all languages will be available in the user's implementation of voice recognition. Thus, before setting a language it is necessary to check whether it is one of the supported languages, and if not, to set the currently preferred language.

To do this, a RecognizerIntent.ACTION_GET_LANGUAGE_DETAILS ordered broadcast is sent that returns a Bundle from which the information about the preferred language (RecognizerIntent.EXTRA_LANGUAGE_PREFERENCE) and the list of supported languages (RecognizerIntent.EXTRA_SUPPORTED_LANGUAGES) can be extracted. This involves modifying the ASR.java file a little in the ASRMultilingualLib library.

Now in the `listen` method, there is a check to make sure the language selected is available in the speech recognizer, and then the new `startASR` method is invoked.

The `startASR` method contains basically the same code as in the `listen` method of the previous version of the library, where the `RecognizerIntent` was created to start listening. However, it introduces a new parameter for the intent in which the language used for recognition is specified, as shown in the following code line which is invoked from the `startASR` method:

```
intent.putExtra(RecognizerIntent.EXTRA_LANGUAGE, language);
```

> To check the languages available on your device, you can click on **Google Voice Search/Voice Search Settings**, and click on **Language** to see the full list. The corresponding codes are two-letter lowercase ISO 639-1 language codes as specified in http://en.wikipedia.org/wiki/List_of_ISO_639-1_codes.

The `listen` method has been changed to check the availability of the language. In order to do so, it uses an intent `RecognizerIntent.ACTION_GET_LANGUAGE_DETAILS`, which is broadcast. To deal with the broadcast, two new classes to the `ASRMultilingualLib` have been introduced: `LanguageDetailsChecker`, which is the `BroadCastReceiver`, and `OnLanguageDetailsListener`, an interface used to specify the method that processes the results of the broadcast. These classes, which handle the details of retrieving language-related information, are from the `gast-lib` project (https://github.com/gast-lib) and are described in the book *Professional Android™ Sensor Programming* by *Greg Milette* and *Adam Stroud*, *Wrox, 2012*. In the `listen` method, the broadcast intent is created and sent, and the `OnLanguageDetailsListener` interface is used to specify what to do when the broadcast has been processed. In our case there is a check to see whether the language matches any of the available ones and then the recognition is started.

After we have made the described changes in the `ASRLib`, we are ready to develop apps in which the user specifies a language in which speech is recognized and synthesized. As an example, we have developed the `SillyParrot` app, as shown in the following figure. It asks for a language and on recognizing what the user wants, plays back the best match in the language selected.

After trying the `SillyParrot` app, you might have noticed that it is a bit strange that the GUI remains in English after you have selected another language. We will go further into the synchronization of the visual and oral parts of the app in the section about multimodality, but we will start now by making sure they are both in the same language. In order to do that, we will take advantage of the `res` folder, which holds `xml` files that contain information that can be referenced from the activities.

The process of implementing an app which is responsive to different languages is usually described as localization of an application. One of the main issues in localization is to provide text messages in different languages, but images, layouts and other resources can also be localized (take a look at the tutorial in this web page to see an example with localized images: `http://www.icanlocalize.com/site/tutorials/android-application-localization-tutorial/`). To do this it is necessary to include the files in specific directories that indicate the language code.

If the locale of a device is `es-ES` and the code makes reference to the string `R.string.mymessage`, Android will look for it in the following directories, in the specified order:

1. `res/values-es-rES/strings.xml`
2. `res/values-es/strings.xml`
3. `res/values/strings.xml`

Thus, if you are in Mexico and the default locale of your device is `es-MX`, then it will not match the default Spanish from Spain (option 1), but it will match the generic Spanish (option 2). If you are in Chicago and the locale of your device is `en-US`, then it will try to find the string in the default directory (option 3).

Don't forget default resources!

We cannot expect that all locales are available in our user's devices (see an explanation here `http://developer.android.com/reference/java/util/Locale.html`), thus it is very important not to forget the default resources, as Android will load them from `res/values/` whenever there is no xml file available for the desired locale.

A good design practice is to include all messages in the target language in the default folder, where it is the one that we expect most users will employ, and then try to create as few resource files as possible for the other languages.

Say, for example, we have identified that our app must support the following languages: English as spoken in US and Canada, Spanish as spoken in US, and French as spoken in Canada, with US English being the main language. In this case, the strings in US English should be in the default folder (`res/values/strings.xml`). Then, only specific messages that are different in Canadian English would be included in a `res/values/en-rCA/strings.xml` folder, so there is no need to replicate all the strings for both locales. A similar process happens with Spanish and French, which can be included in `res/values-ES/` and `res/values-fr/` folders, and later be localized to `res/values-es-rUS` or `res/values-fr-rCA/` if other varieties need to be considered. Android provides a checklist to plan how to localize your apps, which you can find at: `http://developer.android.com/distribute/googleplay/publish/localizing.html`. Pay attention to include the `r` before the country code as well as using `-` instead of `_` when creating the directories.

In the `Parrot` app we have improved `SillyParrot` by automatically adapting to the device locale (`Locale.getDefault().getDisplayLanguage();`) following the structure described in the previous paragraph. Take a look at the directory structure of the project in the code bundle. In the Android developers guide (`http://developer.android.com/guide/topics/resources/localization.htm`) there are examples of how to test localized apps in different languages, though you will need to try with different languages in a physical device to test the speech recognition part.

Multimodality

An application may be considered multimodal if it uses several input and/or output modalities. In this sense, all the apps presented in this book are multimodal, as they use voice as well as a GUI either in the output or input.

However, in the previous examples the modalities were not synchronized or used to provide alternative ways for handling the same bits of information. For example, in the `MusicBrain` app in *Chapter 5, Form-filling Dialogs* the input was oral and the output visual, and in the `SimpleParrot` app described in this chapter, the input and output are oral (requiring speech recognition and synthesis) and visual (selecting a language and the **push to speak** button in the input and **toasts** for output), but they correspond to different elements in the interface.

In this section, we will describe how to develop multimodal applications in which the modalities can be seamlessly combined to input or output data, so the user can select the most convenient modality to use at any particular time.

To do so, we build on the `FormFillLib` library presented in *Chapter 5, Form-filling Dialogs*, augmenting it by considering the synchronization of the oral fields with different elements in the GUI. This way, the user can fill in all the different elements in the GUI by either clicking or using speech.

The main idea is to create a correspondence between the fields in the voice form and the different elements in the GUI. We have considered the combinations of voice and GUI elements shown in the following table, so that when one of the elements in the pair is filled, the other is assigned a value accordingly. For example, if the user is prompted to choose an option and does it orally, the corresponding radio button or element in a list will be selected in the GUI. Similarly, if the element is chosen in the radio button or list, the user will not be asked for it orally.

Description	Voice Field	GUI Element
Open input in which the user may write a long text or provide it orally	The results from the Google Speech Recognizer can be used directly	Text field (`EditText`)
Restricted input in which the user may select between alternative options	A hand-crafted grammar should be used to restrict the options	Group of radio buttons (`RadioGroup`) or lists (`ListView` or `Spinner`)
Restricted yes/no type inputs	A hand-crafted grammar should be used to restrict the options to yes/ no and equivalents (for example, `true`/`false`)	Check boxes (`CheckBox`)

As can be observed in the table, it is important to introduce grammars, because the speech input must only accept the options provided by the GUI. This is why we have also augmented the capabilities of the VXML parser presented in *Chapter 5, Form-Filling Dialogs* to take grammars into account.

In order to do this, the new `MultimodalFormFillLib` library (see `sandra.libs.dm.multimodalformfilllib` in the code bundle) incorporates several changes with respect to the `FormFillLib` library, which are also pointed out as comments in the code bundle. The next figure shows an activity diagram summarizing how oral dialogs are interpreted in the new library. The shaded parts are the main changes with respect to the interpreter presented in *Chapter 5, Form-filling Dialogs*.

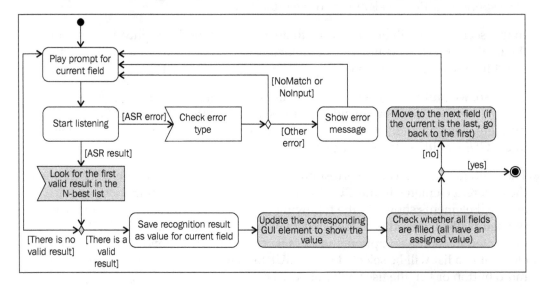

As can be observed in the preceding diagram, in the `MultimodalFormFillLib` library not all recognition results are considered valid in all situations. If we look at the table introduced previously; if an oral field corresponds to a radio button, check box or list in the GUI, we should restrict the valid values for the field to the options provided. For example, if our app presents a selection list of ice-cream flavors containing chocolate, vanilla, and strawberry, then the only valid recognition results when the user is asked what flavor he prefers should be one of those three. This way, the user can either select a flavor on the screen or say the flavor orally, and the app will automatically update the other modality (fill the oral field or select an option in the GUI respectively).

This restriction is implemented by means of grammars. Now, each field contains information about its grammar wherever one has been indicated (for example, there is no need to indicate a grammar for text fields with an unrestricted input). When the field is visited by the `DialogInterpreter`, if there is a grammar, the recognized phrase is only considered if it is valid in the grammar; if not, it is treated as a no match.

For simplicity, we only consider whether the value is valid or not according to the grammar, and not its semantic value. However, this could be done if the isValid method in the Field class did not compute only a Boolean value, but processed the semantics in some way (for example, by following the guidelines presented in *Chapter 6, Grammars for Dialog*).

In VXMLParser.java file, we have included <grammar> as a possible tag to be parsed. This tag has a mandatory src attribute indicating its location. When the parser encounters the tag, it invokes the setGrammar method in the Field class, passing the grammar src as a parameter. In Field.java, we have included methods to retrieve the XML contents of the grammar and to parse and query them. The setGrammar method invokes retrieveGrammar, which accesses the url (the src attribute contained a URL) or reads the grammar from the assets folder (the src attribute contained just the name of the grammar) and obtains the contents in a String. Then the processXMLContents method initializes the handcrafted grammar using the library NLULib developed in *Chapter 6, Grammars for Dialog*. If no grammar is indicated for a specific field, then any recognition result is accepted without subsequent filtering.

We have added another method in Field.java file called isValid, which can be used to check whether a phrase is valid in the grammar. When no grammar is used, the isValid method returns true regardless of the value.

The behavior described is coded in the processAsrResults method of the DialogInterpreter class, in which we have included the code to check if any of the recognition results in the N-best list obtained by the recognizer is valid in the grammar. If so, then the process moves to the next field, if not, it remains in the same field.

When we used the speech-only interface in previous chapters, there was no possibility for the user to delete one of the fields for which he had already provided information. This is not the case with a multimodal interface, as the user may change already provided items in the GUI. We have changed the method moveToNextField in the DialogInterpreter class, so that the condition for the end of the dialog is not that all fields have been visited, but that all fields are filled (their value is not null). The method that checks whether all fields in a form are filled (allFieldsFilled) has been included in the Form class. Also, it considers the list of fields to be circular, so that, when the last field is encountered, if there are unfilled fields it continues with the first.

Now that grammars are ready to be considered, we can look at multimodality. We have created the `MultimodalDialogInterpreter` class, a subclass of `DialogInterpreter` that contains a collection of `MultimodalElement` objects. These objects contain pairs of oral and GUI fields that must be synchronized.

Firstly, we make sure that the changes in the oral part have an impact in the GUI. The method `oraltoGui` (abstract in `DialogInterpreter`, implemented in `MultimodalDialogInterpreter`) is invoked each time a field is filled orally (see the `processResults` method in `DialogInterpreter`) in order to show its value in the GUI. This method checks the type of visual element that corresponds to the oral field and shows the information accordingly by invoking the corresponding method. In list views and spinners it selects one item, in a radio group it checks one of the radio buttons, in a text field it writes a text, or it selects or deselects a checkbox as described in the previous table showing combinations of voice fields and GUI elements.

Secondly, we make sure that the changes in the visual part have an impact in the oral part. Thus if an element has been filled in the GUI, the app should not ask for it orally. The `guiToOral` method in the `MultimodalDialogInterpreter` class is invoked to save the values retrieved from the GUI in the oral fields.

As an example of the use of the `MultimodalFormFillLib`, we present the `SendMessage` app, shown in the next figure, in which the user fills some pieces of information either orally, or using the GUI, or with both. It is a mock app, as it does not read the contacts from the user's contacts list and does not send any message, as the focus of this chapter is on the interface. However this can be done following the instructions provided here: `http://developer.android.com/training/contacts-provider/retrieve-names.html` and using the `SMSManager` for sending SMS, or an Intent with `ACTION_SEND` and `EXTRA_EMAIL` to send e-mails by just changing the implementation of the `populateContactList` and `sendMessage` methods in `SendMessage.java` file.

The `SendMessage` app reads the VXML file that contains the structure of the oral dialog from the `assets` folder as shown in the following code:

```
<form>

<field name="contact">
<prompt>Who is the recipient?</prompt>
<grammar src="contact_grammar.xml"/>
<noinput> Sorry, I could not hear you </noinput>
<nomatch> Sorry, I did not understand what you said. Please say
    the name of one of your contacts </nomatch>
</field>

<field name="ack">
<grammar src="ack_grammar.xml"/>
<prompt>Do you need acknowledgment of receipt?</prompt>
<noinput> Sorry, I could not hear you </noinput>
<nomatch> Sorry, I did not understand what you said </nomatch>
</field>

<field name="urgency">
<grammar src="urgency_grammar.xml"/>
<prompt>Is the message urgent or normal?</prompt>
<noinput> Sorry, I could not hear you </noinput>
<nomatch> Sorry, I did not understand what you said </nomatch>
</field>

<field name="message">
<prompt>Please dictate the message</prompt>
<noinput> Sorry, I could not hear you </noinput>
</field>

</form>
```

As can be observed in the VXML file and the GUI, there are four pieces of information required from the user; the recipient, whether he wants an acknowledgment of receipt, the urgency of the message (normal or urgent), and the message to be sent. We have used all the different GUI elements supported. As can be observed in the VXML code, all fields have grammars assigned except for the message. The `contact_grammar` accepts the contact names, the `ack_grammar` accepts phrases that can be translated to Boolean values such as `yes`, `no`, `true`, or `false`, the `urgency_grammar` contains the two possible values `normal` and `urgent`, and the `message` field does not indicate a grammar so that it accepts the best recognition result allowing the user to talk freely.

The VXML could also be read from the web as in *Chapter 5, Form-filling Dialogs,* but as it is so coupled with the GUI it is unlikely to change much, so it can be stored more conveniently in the assets folder. For example, we take into account that the valid values for the oral input are the same as the options shown visually in the GUI. In the previous screenshot, the radio buttons show the text **Normal** and **Urgent**, and thus, the corresponding oral field should only accept the values urgent and normal. Developers must bear in mind that this poses a considerable restriction on the VXML and grammar files.

The SendMessage class is a subclass of MultimodalDialogInterpreter. In the onCreate method it invokes the initializeGUI and startDialog methods. The former initializes all the GUI elements, which must invoke the guiToOral method in their listeners (as the oral part must be changed after the changes in the GUI). The latter parses the oral form, sets the correspondences between the oral and visual elements (setMultimodalCorrespondence), and starts the oral interaction. The oral dialog controls the end of the interaction. When the processDialogResults is invoked, the user is informed about the success of the interaction (in a real setting, this method would actually send the message).

Note that the oral part will not be ready until the vxml file is read and parsed. This is why the GUI must wait for this process to be finished before trying to update the oral part. This is taken into account when setting the GUI elements (in the setContactList, setAckCheckBox, setUrgencyRadioGroup, and setMessageEditText).

The next screenshot shows an excerpt from a sample interaction with the SendMessage app where the final state of the GUI is as shown in the previous screenshot. In the example, the user selects to receive an acknowledgement of receipt and to send the message urgently. This information is saved by the system in the oral fields. As can be observed in the screenshot, the user is not asked for these pieces of information orally. Then, the user speaks the name of the recipient. As it is one of the valid contacts, it is accepted and shown in the GUI in the corresponding selection list.

Finally, the user provides the message, and the result is shown in the GUI without being previously filtered by a grammar as shown in the following screenshot:

Summary

This chapter has shown how to include languages other than English into apps, using resources associated with different locale settings. We also looked at how to synchronize the oral and visual modalities so that users can combine them when interacting with the apps.

In the next chapter we will describe how to design virtual personal assistants that can engage in conversation and perform a range of tasks on your device.

8
Dialogs with Virtual Personal Assistants

In this chapter you will learn how to design and develop three types of **Virtual Personal Assistant (VPA)**; a conversational companion that can chat about a range of everyday topics, a specialist VPA that provides answers to **Frequently Asked Questions (FAQs)** in the domain of Type 2 diabetes, and a conversational companion enhanced with the ability to execute search queries, control device apps, and make calls to web services.

By the end of this chapter, you should have an understanding of what is required to develop each type of VPA.

The technology of VPA

VPAs are generally able to perform the following tasks:

- Interacting with web services to retrieve information and perform transactions; either through search queries, by linking to knowledge bases such as Knowledge Graph, or by engaging in transactional dialogs as well as launching and managing apps on the device, such as contacts, calendar, SMS, or clock.

- Engaging in conversation with the user about random topics, for example, answering questions such as *where do you live?*, *how old are you?*, *what languages do you speak?*, or *what sort of music do you like?*. The VPA is expected to provide some sort of response to every question so as to be able to keep the conversation going even if it does not have a proper answer to the question.

The VoiceLaunch app presented in *Chapter 4, Simple Voice Interactions* shows how to launch an app on a device, while the MusicBrain app presented in *Chapter 5, Form-filling Dialogs* shows how to implement a transactional dialog using form-filling. The multimodal app presented in *Chapter 7, Multilingual and Multimodal Dialogs* showed unimodal as well as multimodal dialogs. However, these apps perform a single task, whereas a VPA performs a range of different tasks.

The challenge for a VPA is to determine from the user's utterance what task the user is requesting. Looking at the data flow in the following figure, we know how to use speech recognition to determine the words that the user has spoken (*Chapter 3, Speech Recognition*), and how to give a response, given a string of words to speak (*Chapter 2, Text-To-Speech Synthesis*). Now, we need to figure out the intention behind the words spoken by the user and put together the words to be spoken by the TTS. Determining the user's intention can be done using techniques from spoken language understanding, as shown in *Chapter 6, Grammars for Dialog*, although in this chapter we will look at an alternative technique. Providing the words to be spoken by the TTS will be explained when we look at how responses are generated by the dialog management component.

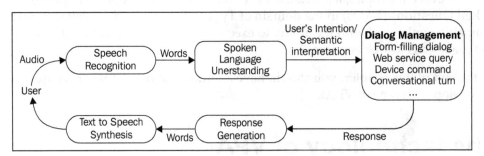

Determining the user's intention

Imagine the following user inputs:

- *I would like to book a flight to London.*
- *What's the weather forecast for tomorrow?*
- *Set my alarm for 7.30 tomorrow.*
- *What sort of a computer are you?*

Suppose we wish to map these inputs on to the four functions listed in the dialog management box in the previous figure. How can we do this?

One way is to use a statistical classification system to classify open-ended user input into a fixed set of classes, as illustrated in the statistical grammar in *Chapter 6, Grammars for Dialog*. This is the approach taken in large scale commercial systems. For example, a troubleshooting application might take inputs such as the following:

- *I can't access my e-mail*
- *I can't get on to the Internet*
- *There's a little icon that says no Internet access*

Although these inputs are phrased differently, they could all be classified as problems to do with Internet connectivity. Creating such a statistical classification system involves collecting a large set of relevant utterances and determining a fixed set of classes. Features such as the occurrence of particular keywords or phrases are identified that can predict the assignment of an utterance to a particular class and machine learning techniques would be employed to train the classifier. For example, the occurrence of phrases such as *access my e-mail* or *get on the Internet* could be taken as features that indicate the class *problem with Internet connection*.

The advantages of this approach are robustness and coverage. As the matching is statistical, it is possible to classify input that might not match a category exactly. Thus, ungrammatical input or input that can be expressed in different ways can still be assigned to a class. Handcrafting a grammar to classify such open-ended input would be a daunting task as in this case, the matching would have to be exact.

The downside of statistical text classification is that a large sample of utterances is required to train the system since there are so many different ways to say something. In a large system, tens of thousands of typical utterances might need to be collected and annotated to provide adequate coverage. This is an expensive process; although once a system has been trained, it will generally produce accurate results.

A second approach, which would be feasible in situations where the input is more constrained and predictable, would be to write grammars to perform the classification, using the techniques illustrated in *Chapter 6, Grammars for Dialog*, and setting the output of the parsing to be an assignment to one of the relevant classes along with associated values. For example, in the case of a command to set an alarm, assigning the output to the device's alarm function and extracting the time and date. However, the problem of coverage also arises with handcrafted grammars and additional rules would have to be continually added to deal with inputs that cannot be parsed with the existing rules.

A third approach, is to match the input against predefined patterns. This approach has been deployed successfully in the implementation of a number of commercially available chatbots and VPAs. The downside is that initially a large number of patterns have to be created to match all the possible inputs, with the same problem of potential lack of coverage.

Making an appropriate response

The app's response to the user's input varies according to the user intention that has been identified, which can be broadly classified into the following categories:

- For form-filling dialogs, the dialog has to be initiated and several rounds of system-user interaction may be required to fill the necessary slots in the dialog's frame, as shown in *Chapter 5, Form-filling Dialogs*

- In the case of web services, the response will be a call to the web service involved and some text will be extracted to be spoken by the TTS

- For tasks involving the activation of features on the device, such as placing a call or setting an alarm, the command is executed and some text is extracted to be spoken by the TTS

- Finally, if the task is conversation, the VPA provides a conversational response which is generated by the Pandorabots chatbot system for the apps presented in this chapter

Pandorabots

Pandorabots is a free open source-based web service that enables developers to create and host chatbots on the web (see http://www.pandorabots.com/). Currently, more than 221,000 chatbots are hosted, covering a range of languages. There is also a premium service for commercial development. Many VPAs on mobile devices have been created using Pandorabots. These include Voice Actions by Pannous (also known as Jeannie), Skyvi, Iris, and Pandorabot's own CallMom app. CallMom can perform the same sorts of tasks as other VPAs, but also includes a learning feature so that it can learn personal preferences and contacts, and can be taught to correct speech recognition errors.

ALICE 2.0 is one of the chatbot personalities available in the `CallMom` app. Its predecessor ALICE, originally developed in 1995 by Dr. Richard S. Wallace, has won numerous awards in chatbot competitions, including the Loebner prize that is awarded to the chatbot, which in an annual competition is considered by judges to be the most human-like. Three of the four finalists in the 2013 Loebner competition used the Pandorabots technology. Much of the knowledge in the original ALICE was hard-wired and has now become obsolete. For example, the response to *Who is the Prime Minister of England?* has not been updated from the original response *Tony Blair*. ALICE 2.0 overcomes these shortcomings by obtaining its factual information from external services, as do other VPAs such as Siri. More information about Pandorabots and chatbots in general can be found at the Pandorabots website and at the ALICE A.I. Foundation site (`www.alicebot.org`), founded by Wallace to promote the development of **Artificial Intelligence Markup Language (AIML)** and chatbot technology in general.

AIML

AIML is an XML-based language used to specify the conversational behaviors of chatbots. The basic unit in AIML is `category`, which consists of a `pattern` and a `template` attribute. The following is an example:

```
<category>
        <pattern> WHAT ARE YOU </pattern>
        <template>
                I am the latest result in artificial intelligence, which
                can reproduce the capabilities of the human brain with
                greater speed and accuracy.
        </template>
</category>
```

In this example, the user's input is matched against the pattern WHAT ARE YOU and the response provided in the template is generated. By using many thousands of categories and wild cards to enable more flexible pattern matching, quite sophisticated conversations can be produced.

Wild cards are used to match a string of one or more words in the input. Here is a simple example of the wildcard `*`:

```
<category>
        <pattern>ABBA *</pattern>
        <template>They were a great band in the 70's.</template>
</category>
```

In this example, any input starting with ABBA will match this category, resulting in the output They were a great band in the 70's.

There are often several different ways of saying the same thing and rather than listing each as a pattern or template pair, the <srai> tag (meaning symbolic reduction) can be used, as in the following example:

```
<category>
        <pattern> HOW DID YOU GET YOUR NAME </pattern>
        <template> <srai>WHAT DOES ALICE STAND FOR </srai> </template>
</category>
```

Here the input HOW DID YOU GET YOUR NAME is treated in meaning to be the same as WHAT DOES ALICE STAND FOR, and the <srai> tag indicates that they should both have the same answer.

If there is no pattern that matches the input; in other words, the bot does not understand what has been said to it; the ultimate default category applies. For this category, the pattern is * and the default response is I have no answer for that. The art of bot programming is to provide a series of responses in the ultimate default category that helps to keep the conversation going. For example, *tell me more about yourself* should cause the user to say something for which there will probably be a matching pattern. The ultimate default category can also be used to catch input that is not predicted by any pattern and process it to determine if it can be handled in some other way. For example, it could be sent to a search engine or an online knowledge source to get a response.

Pattern matching is performed using a matching algorithm that conducts a graph search through the categories. The text in the AIML patterns is first tidied up by removing unnecessary punctuations, converting to upper case, and expanding contractions such as I'll to I will.

As far as templates are concerned, in addition to specifying the text of the response, it is also possible to perform simple computations. For example, values of properties, which are constants referring to properties of the bot, such as age, name, or location, can be retrieved. There are methods for dealing with predicates also, which are variables set during a conversation for items such as the topic of the conversation, or how to deal with the use of pronouns to refer to a particular word. These computations help to make the conversation more natural.

A more comprehensive coverage of AIML is beyond the scope of this book. Full documentation can be found at the Pandorabots website (www.pandorabots.com).

Using oob tag to add additional functions

The `<oob>` tag is a recent addition to AIML that supports usage on mobile devices. OOB stands for *out of band*, a term taken from engineering to refer to a conversation on a separate, hidden channel. In AIML, `<oob>` tags can be used to send commands to the device, for example, to place a call, send a text message, launch an app, and so on. The content of the tag is not a part of the response received by the user, so items such as URLs, app names, and other keywords can be included here to be extracted and treated as desired in the Android code. Here are a few examples of patterns using the `<oob>` tag:

```
<category>
      <pattern> * </pattern>
      <template>
            <oob><url><search><star/></search></url></oob>
            Please wait while I try to find an answer from Google
      </template>
</category>
```

In this example, if the bot does not find a match for the user's input in its AIML files, the response is marked as `<search>`. The content of the search query is `<star/>`, the value of which is the words spoken in the input. The code to carry out this stage for this and the following examples can be found in VPALib in the code bundle (`sandra. libs.vpa.vpalib`). The text located outside the `<oob>` tag can be used for other purposes; in these apps, it is sent to TTS and used for the spoken output.

The following example shows how the input WIKIPEDIA sets up the launch of the URL for Wikipedia:

```
<category>
      <pattern>WIKIPEDIA</pattern>
      <template>
            <oob><url>http://www.wikipedia.org</url></oob>
            Opening Wikipedia
      </template>
</category>
```

In the following example, the matched input GMAIL sets up the launch of Google mail:

```
<category>
      <pattern>GMAIL</pattern>
      <template>
            <oob><launch>com.google.android.gm</launch></oob>
            Launching Gmail.
      </template>
</category>
```

The VPALib library

We have created a library that contains the code which connects with Pandorabots. Any app that wants to incorporate an agent just has to deal with the interface aspects, such as the GUI appearance and the control of the speech recognition and synthesis.

The VPALib library uses ASRLib, TTSLib, and XMLLib to manage speech recognition, speech synthesis, and asynchronous tasks when retrieving web contents (you can see it if you check the libs folder in the VPALib project). This way, it can focus on the code required to manage the VPA behavior.

The main class in the VPALib library is the Bot class, which sends queries to the Pandorabots website, parses the results, and carries out the corresponding actions on the device.

When a new bot is created, we must specify an ID to the constructor. This is the ID in the Pandorabots site (for example, d7b695cf0e344c0a for Jack). Also, we can specify its topic of specialization. For example, if the bot is specialized for providing information about the NFL, the string NFL is used to carry out web searches. So, if the user asks for games, the bot searches for NFL games, and not any kind of games.

The initiateQuery method sends a text corresponding to the user input, to the bot on the Pandorabots site. This process involves inserting %20 for spaces in the query, as the values posted need to be form-URL encoded, creating the query and sending it as a background asynchronous task to Pandorabots, using the XMLLib folder described in *Chapter 5, Form-filling Dialogs*.

The results from AsyncTask are processed in the processXMLContents() method. The output from the response that comes back from Pandorabots is parsed using XMLPullParser in a similar way to how we parsed VXML (*Chapter 5, Form-filling Dialogs*) or XML grammar files (*Chapter 6, Grammars for Dialog*).

The response either includes <oob> tags or does not. If it does not, the only task for the bot is to parse and synthesize the response. For this, it must extract the message contained within the <that> tag. Here is an example of the outcome of AsyncTask:

```
<result status="0" botid=" d7b695cf0e344c0a"
custid="c6015de7be06c599">
        <input> what languages do you speak </input>
        <that> C, Java, Lisp, SETL and English </that>
</result>
```

In this case, the method would invoke the TTS engine to synthetize C, Java, Lisp, SETL and English.

 The gender of Google's TTS voices cannot be programmatically selected. We have used the UK English voice, which is currently male, but it might be possible that the gender selected for the VPA does not match the voice in the user's device. Currently, this can only be resolved by using other TTS engines.

When <oob> tags are present, we assume that they have been marked up in the AIML file with one of the tags: <search>, <launch>, <url>, and <dial>. When <search> is encountered, the googleQuery method is invoked, which launches a query in Google search engines. When <launch> is encountered, the launchApp method is invoked that launches an app in the device. Similarly, the launchUrl method is invoked when the <url> tag is encountered to open the specified web page. Finally, when <dial> is processed, it invokes the placePhoneCall method, which dials a number.

The launchApp and launchUrl methods are similar to those introduced in *Chapter 4, Simple Voice Interactions*, except that there the code was more complex as it used similarity functions. The methods shown in this chapter have been kept simpler in order to focus on the use of <oob> tags as a technique for recognizing these commands within the user's input.

More generally, it is up to the developer to decide whether to mark up the different functions in AIML and then process them or whether to employ a different method for recognizing whether the output is text to be spoken or a command to be executed.

Creating a Pandorabot

The apps that will be described in the following sections use AIML code provided on the Pandorabots site. Thus, the first step we must take is to register for an account in the Pandorabots website.

Once registered, enter the site and click on the **Create a Pandorabot** option. This will open a page where you will be asked to name your bot (we called ours Jack). Select your startup AIML from a number of choices, including an option of **No initial content, the Pandorabot starts with no knowledge**. For the purposes of this example, select one of the AIML sets (for example, **Dr Wallace's A.L.I.C.E – March 2002**). This will take you to a page for your Pandorabot where you can explore a number of options.

To see the AIML files, click on **AIML** and then on any of the files listed. This will give an idea of the large number of categories that can be used to provide conversational responses.

To try out the bot with the pre-existing AIML, click on Train and then ask questions to see what responses the bot gives. This will bring up a training page indicating the AIML file where a match has been found for your input as well as various other options that help to refine the bot. The pre-existing AIML files cannot be modified but any new categories will be stored in a file called update.aiml.

To enable your bot to be available for others to use, you must publish it (or republish, if you have made any changes to the AIML code). Return to the home page of your bot and click on **Publish**. This will load a page showing the location of your bot.

Clicking on this link will open a page that is available publicly to anyone who has access to the link, letting them interact with your bot. In this way, you can collect further data from interactions with the bot and view them in log files, enabling you to further refine the bot's responses.

In this example, we will provide an interface that runs on an Android device and uses speech to interact with the bot. It will be important to note the **botid**, as this will be required when connecting to your bot from your Android program.

Sample VPAs – Jack, Derek, and Stacy

To illustrate the use of VPALib, we have developed three bots: Jack, Derek, and Stacy. As can be observed in their respective packages (see the code bundle), they have the same structure; a main activity that implements ASR and TTS and creates an instance of the bot, and a simple graphical interface. This shows the convenience of having a library that deals with the connection to Pandorabots. The main difference is in their corresponding AIML files.

The links in Pandorabots for the bots are as follows:

- Jack: http://www.pandorabots.com/pandora/talk?botid=d7b695cf0e344c0a

- Derek: http://www.pandorabots.com/pandora/talk?botid=a80ce25abe344199

- Stacy: http://www.pandorabots.com/pandora/talk?botid=e257c70bae346e98

The interfaces for Jack and Derek are shown in the following screenshot:

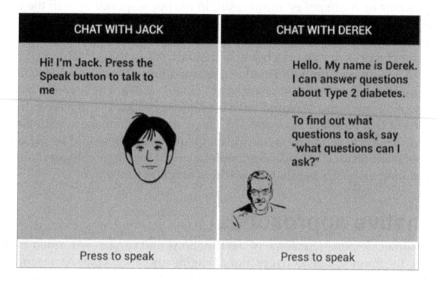

Jack is a general-purpose VPA, while Derek is a specialized VPA. Specialized VPAs perform tasks such as providing customer service or answering customer queries. The VPA's knowledge base is encoded in AIML as a set of question-response pairs, similar to FAQs. We have developed a rudimentary set of questions in AIML about Type 2 diabetes. Derek can answer questions about topics such as symptoms, causes, treatment, risks to children, and complications.

Stacy has the same AIML files as Jack but in addition, has a file containing categories with <oob> tags to perform a small selection of functions such as the following:

- Sending a search term to DBPedia, obtaining a response, and speaking it. If no text is available from DBPedia, the search term is sent to Google search.

- Calling a web page (Wikipedia or Facebook).

- Launching an app on the device (clock, calendar, phone).

The code to perform these functions can be found in VPALib in the code bundle.

Notice in the Jack.java (Jack project) and Derek.java (Derek project) files how the Bot class is instantiated differently. In the case of Jack, it is without specializedTopic, while in the case of Derek, it is Type 2 diabetes, using the two alternative constructors of the Bot class (VPALib project).

After running the `Derek` app a few times, it will soon become apparent that misrecognitions of your spoken input result in the bot responding with the default response `I have no answer for that`. This is likely to become annoying after a few times but there is also the problem that a potentially valid query is lost because the recognized words do not match any of the patterns in the AIML code. For example, in one interaction with Derek we said *what are the risks to my children* and the app returned the recognition result `what other risks children`, which did not match any of our patterns. It would have been more productive to have extracted the useful parts of this phrase, `risks` and `children`, and combine them with the term `Type 2 diabetes`, to send an expanded search query which would be more likely to find a relevant result. This has been implemented by using a category in the AIML code containing an `<oob>` tag that links with a function in `VPALib`.

Alternative approaches

These examples demonstrate some of the functions that can be performed by a VPA using the Pandorabots conversational engine and `<oob>` tags as a resource. Other functions can be added too (for a complete list of `<oob>` tags with examples, see `https://code.google.com/p/aiml-en-us-pandorabots-callmom/wiki/CallMomOOBTags`).

The following are some limitations to this approach:

- For general conversational interaction, there should to be sufficient default responses to handle cases when there is no match for the input. This is not a serious problem as there are lots of examples in the pre-existing AIML code that can be used or adapted.

- In the case of specialized VPAs, it might not be sufficient to use the rather adhoc procedure of sending unmatched input to a search engine, even if the query is expanded, as in the previous example, where the words `Type 2 diabetes` were added to the search query. This approach relies very much on the search engine coming back with a list of URLs that fit in with the user's query and on the search text reflecting accurately the user's intended query.

- The use of `<oob>` tags depends on creating patterns that correctly match the user's input. For example, the user should say something like *calendar*, *Gmail*, or some other keyword to indicate which device function is intended. These patterns in the AIML code have to be closely linked to the Java code that makes use of them. A library that implements this would be a useful addition.

- The approach does not generalize easily for websites. For example, each website, such as Wikipedia, has to be coded separately as a pattern in a category in AIML.

A more sophisticated and scalable method for determining the user's intention could be to use the types of grammar illustrated in *Chapter 6, Grammars for Dialog*. A handcrafted grammar could be designed to recognize key words or phrases in the input, or an appropriate statistical grammar could be developed to handle the input more robustly. Input that is not extracted in this way could then be treated as conversational input and passed to a resource such as AIML.

Some of these issues are being addressed by the Pandorabots team but the solutions are not currently available as open source code. New developments will be posted on the website for the book.

Summary

In this chapter we have seen how to develop different types of VPAs using the resources provided by the Pandorabots chatbot technology. Based on the apps described here, you should now be able to design and develop VPAs for your own purposes. Some suggestions for how to build on these examples and to include more of the techniques described throughout the book are presented in *Chapter 9, Taking it Further*.

9
Taking it Further

During the course of this book you have learned how to use the Google Speech APIs and to apply a range of techniques as shown in the apps described in *Chapter 8, Dialogs with Virtual Personal Assistants*. However, to keep these apps reasonably simple, some of the more advanced techniques were not utilized. This chapter suggests ways in which these techniques can be included in a more advanced virtual personal assistant.

Developing a more advanced Virtual Personal Assistant

The **system output**, which uses TTS as presented in *Chapter 2, Text-to-speech synthesis* could be enhanced by including the use of different voices, languages, and modalities, for example, to present information that is less suitable for spoken output.

The **user input** techniques for speech recognition that were introduced in *Chapter 3, Speech Recognition* could be developed in various ways:

- By including the similarity measures introduced in *Chapter 4, Simple Voice Interactions* to compare the recognized results with similar words that might have been what the user actually said

- By making use of other techniques for enhancing the recognition results, such as stemming, as described in *Chapter 17* of the book *Professional Android Sensor Programming* by *Greg Milette* and *Adam Stroud*

- By incorporating confidence measures to support decisions on whether to use confirmations, as described in *Chapter 4, Simple Voice Interactions*

- By making use of the n-best recognition results to determine whether one of the results is more plausible than the first-best recognition result

- By allowing for input in other languages, as described in *Chapter 7, Multilingual and Multimodal Apps*

- By switching to other modalities if speech recognition has become unreliable or otherwise problematic (see *Chapter 7, Multilingual and Multimodal Apps*)

Interpretation of the user's input by the apps presented in *Chapter 8, Dialogs with Virtual Personal Assistants,* in which simple pattern matching of the user's input with the pattern in an AIML category was used and the app's response was retrieved from the template of that category. Oob tags were used to pick up keywords such as search or URL in order to activate actions such as searching or launching a web page. A more advanced approach to the analysis of the user's input would involve filtering it using the techniques described in *Chapter 6, Grammars for Dialog,* by developing grammars to parse the response returned by the speech recognition engine and classifying it into different types.

The selection of the app's next action by **dialog management** and its verbal responses could be improved in various ways as indicated in the following:

- Form-filling was not implemented in the apps presented in *Chapter 8, Dialogs with Virtual Personal Assistants.* Including form-filling dialogs, as described in *Chapter 5, Form-filling Dialogs,* and *Chapter 7, Multilingual and Multimodal Apps,* would recognize a user input such as *I want to book a hotel in Barcelona* as a request for a transaction and the appropriate form-filling dialog would be launched to handle it.

- Additional knowledge sources could be added such as the use of a knowledge source such as Freebase to support question answering. Freebase is the open core of Google's Knowledge Graph. Documentation and instructions on how to obtain an API key can be found at the website `https://developers.google.com/freebase/`.

Currently the **user interface** is a combination of speech input and output and a traditional graphical user interface. Many commercial sites use talking-head technology (or avatars) to provide a persona for their VPA. A worthwhile enhancement would be to build a VPA that includes a talking head and also includes personal information to give the VPA a persona. There are several options available, some of which are referenced on the Pandorabots site (`http://www.pandorabots.com/`).

Summary

This chapter has presented various suggestions for extending the examples presented in this book. You are encouraged to test, modify, and play with the code provided in the book. In the website for the book at `http://lsi.ugr.es/zoraida/androidspeechbook` you will find the source for the code, as well as further ideas for new projects, and a variety of interesting resources and updates. Voice technology is an exciting topic that offers an ocean of possibilities to Android developers. We invite you to take a deep breath and immerse yourself in it!

Afterword

Now that you have read this book, you know how to implement applications that speak and listen. Begin by developing small personal applications that you can show your friends and relatives. You can also show the applications to prospective employers or clients. Some small personal applications that my students have implemented are below. Build one of these applications to demonstrate what you can do with speech technologies on Android mobile devices.

Interactive greeting card

Deliver your message not only via text, but also voice (a recorded voice sounds more personalized than synthesized voice). Collect responses from the person receiving the greeting card and e-mail them to yourself.

Interactive recipe

Present recipe ingredients and instructions for preparing a dish verbally, as well as visually, to assist preparation. The cook verbally navigates through the instructions. One student replaced synthesized instructions with verbal instructions recorded by her grandmother. So the instructions for baking grandma's apple pie are presented in grandma's actual voice. Sweet!

Choose your own adventure story

Record snippets of a fairy tale in your own voice. Insert voice menus between snippets that ask the listener to choose the next snippet. Your children can listen to you telling them bedtime stories, and direct the actions taken by the story characters.

Verbal flash cards

Pose brief questions to listeners, who respond by speaking the answers. Great for learning times tables, names of important people, dates in history, and words in a foreign language.

Call answering system

Ask callers questions about the purposes of their calls and with whom they want to speak. Use this application to filter your telephone calls and record messages for specific members of your household.

Travel guide

Use the GPS API to determine where your mobile device is, and to add photos, graphics, and landmark descriptions that the users can see. Use the GPS API to locate the mobile phone and read/display information about its current location. Or virtually explore places where you cannot go. One student developed a travel guide of the universe using photos from NASA.

Audio commentaries

Add commentary to your photo albums, your recent trip, a wedding you attended, even your son or daughter's ball game.

Show your creativity Enhance your existing applications or create new ones with speech technologies. If you are a student, submit your speech application to the **Applied Voice Input/Output Society (AVIOS)** student contest `http://www.avios.org/`. Submit your speech application to the Google Store, `https://play.google.com/store`. Show the world what you can do!

James A. Larson

Vice President and Founder of Larson Technical Services

Index

Symbols

\<dial> tag 95
\<grammar> tag 63, 68
\<item> tag 68
\<one-of> tag 63, 68
\<oob> tag
  used, for adding additional functions 93
\<ruleref> tag 68
\<rule> tag 68
\<search> tag 95
\<srai> tag 92
\<tag> tag 66, 68
\<that> tag 94
\<url> tag 95

A

acoustic model 24
ACTION_CHECK_TTS_DATA() method
    18
ACTION_RECOGNIZE_SPEECH action 27
ADC 23
additional functions
  adding, \<oob> tag used 93
advanced Virtual Personal Assistant
  developing 101, 102
AIML
  about 91, 92
  example 91
  \<oob> tag, using to add additional
      functions 93
  URL 92
Album class 58
ALICE A.I. Foundation site
  URL 91
Alternative class 69
analogue-to-digital converter. See ADC
Android device
  speech, using on 7-10
Android speech-based apps
  Android Voice Actions 8, 9
  speech-to-text 7
  TTS 8
  Voice Search 8
  VPA 9-11
Android Voice Actions
  about 8
  call businesses 9
  call contacts 9
  get directions 9
  go to websites 9
  search google 9
  Send text messages 9
  view a map 9
app response
  creating 90
Arguments tab 39
articulatory synthesis 16
Artificial Intelligence Markup Language. See
    AIML
ASR 23
ASRBegin app 29
ASR class 32
ASRLib library 57
ASRMultilingualLib library 75
ASRWithIntent app
  about 26
  optional extras 28
  screenshot 27
  speech recognition, supporting 27, 28
  working 29, 30

ASRWithLib app 33
  about 31
  working 31-33
ASRWithLib class 33
AsyncTask
  about 50
  URL 50
AT&T Speech Mashup
  URL 12
Augmented BNF (ABNF) 62
Automatic Speech Recognition. *See* ASR

B

Bot class 94, 97
botid 96

C

call keyword 9
Chatbots 10
Check ASR button 72
CheckBox element 79
Check text button 72
compareOrthographic method 42
comparePhonetic method 42
ComparisonTest java project 39
computeRegularExpression method 69
com.voicedemos package 42
concatenative speech synthesis 17
confirmation scenario 43
createAlert() method 58
Create a Pandorabot option 95
createRecognizer method 31
currentPosition 53

D

depart_time rule 70
Derek bot
  about 96-98
  interface 97
  URL 96
DEVELOPERS tab 71
DialogInterpreter class 53, 80, 81
dialog management
  used, for app action selecting 102

Dialog systems 10
doInBackground() method 50

E

ECAs 10
EditText element 79
Email application 38
Embodied conversational agents. *See* ECAs
END_TAG event 52
equals() method 58
exception attribute 50
EXTRA_LANGUAGE option 29
EXTRA_MAX_RESULTS option 28
EXTRA_PROMPT option 28

F

Field class 51, 81
filterAlbums() method 58
flight_query element 63
formant synthesis 16
Form class 51, 81
form-filling dialog
  about 47
  example 47, 48
  implementing 48, 49
FormFillLib
  about 51, 52
  DialogInterpreter 53, 54
  using, illustration 55-58
  VXMLParser 52
FormFillLibException class 52
FormFillLib library 79, 80
Form Interpretation Algorithm (FIA) 49
Form object 52
Frequently Asked Questions (FAQs) 87

G

getRegExpr() method 70
getSimilarAppsSorted method 39, 40
getStringArrayListExtra method 30
getText() method 21
googleQuery method 95
Google speech
  prefering, reasons 11

Google speech recognition
screenshot 24
using 24, 25
Google speech recognition API
applications, developing with 25-33
Google speech recognition API applications
ASRWithIntent app 26-30
ASRWithLib app 31-33
Google speech recognition service 24
Google TTS
applications, developing with 19, 20
TTS engine, starting 18, 19
using 17-19
Google TTS applications
TTSReadFile app 20
TTSWithLib app 19, 20
go to key phrase 9
GrammarElement class 69
Grammar Specification Language (GSL) 62
GrammarTest app
about 72
screenshot 73
grammers
hand-crafted grammars 61
statistical grammars 61
used, for NLU 62
used, for speech recognition 61
group attribute 71
groupCount attribute 71
GUI elements
CheckBox 79
EditText 79
ListView 79
RadioGroup 79
guiToOral method 82, 84

H

HandCraftedGrammar class 69, 70
HandCraftedGrammar constructor 69
hand-crafted grammars
using, for NLU 62-66
Hidden Markov Model 24

I

information types, Maluuba API
action 67

category 67
entities 67
initializeGUI method 84
initiateQuery method 94
interpretCurrentField() method 53
isValid method 81
Item class 69

J

Jack bot
about 96-98
interface 97
URL 96
Java Script Grammar Format (JSGF) 62
java.util.regex API 69
JVoiceXML
URL 49

K

KEY attribute 72

L

LANGUAGE_MODEL_FREE_FORM model 62
LANGUAGE_MODEL_FREE_FORM option 28
language models
about 24
LANGUAGE_MODEL_FREE_FORM 62
LANGUAGE_MODEL_WEB_SEARCH 62
LANGUAGE_MODEL_WEB_SEARCH model 62
LANGUAGE_MODEL_WEB_SEARCH option 28
launchApp method 39, 42, 95
launchintent 42
launchUrl method 95
Levenshtein distance
computing 42
LevenshteinDistance.java class 42
listen() method 27, 31, 32, 76
ListView element 79
ListView method 30

M

Maluuba API
  example 67
  information, extracting 67
  URL 67
Matcher class 69
message field 83
moveToNextField() method 53, 81
multilingual dialogs 75-78
MultimodalDialogInterpreter class 82, 84
multimodal dialogs 79-84
MultimodalFormFillLib library 80
MusicBrain app
  about 55, 79
  developing 55, 56
  screenshot 56
  working 57, 58
MusicBrainParser class 58
MusicBrainZ API
  URL 56
MyApp class 40, 41
myASR attribute 31

N

nAPI. *See* **Maluuba API**
N-best list 24
negation scenario 43
next() method 52
NLU
  grammers, using 62
  hand-crafted grammers, using 62-66
NLULib 68
noinput event 53
nomatch event 53
Nuance Grammar Builder
  using 62

O

obtainSemantics method 71
onActivityResult handler 19
onActivityResult() method 27
onActivityResults(int, int, Intent) method 29
onAsrReadyForSpeech method 33

onBeginningOfSpeech event 31
onBufferReceived event 31
onClickListener() method 21
onCreate method 84
onDestroy() method 20
onEndOfSpeech event 31
onError event 31
onEvent event 31
OnInitListener interface 18
onInit() method 18
OnLanguageDetailsListener interface 76
onPartialResults event 31
onPostExecute() method 50
onPreExecute() method 50
onProgressUpdate() method 50
onReadyForSpeech event 31
onResults event 31
onResults method 33
onRmsChanged event 31
oraltoGui method 82
orthographic similarity 38

P

PackageManager class 31
Pandorabots
  about 90
  AIML 91-93
  creating 95, 96
  URL 90
  using 90, 91
Pandorabots site
  URL 102
Parrot app 78
parse method 68, 69
parseMusicResults() method 58
parseVXML() method 52
pattern attribute 91
Pattern class 69
phonetic distance
  computing 42
phonetic similarity 39
placePhoneCall method 95
populateContactList method 82
pre-recorded speech
  demerits 17

Press the button to speak option 36
processAsrErrors() method 53
processAsrResults() method 33, 37, 53, 81
processDialogResult() method 57
processDialogResults() method 54, 57
processResults method 39, 40, 43, 82
processXMLContents() method 51, 57, 81, 94
push to speak button 79

Q

QUEUE_ADD parameter 18
QUEUE_FLUSH parameter 18

R

RadioGroup element 79
RecognitionListener interface 31
RecognizerIntent approach 25, 26
RecognizerIntent class 27-31
RecognizerIntent.EXTRA_RESULTS parameter 30
repeat attribute 64
Repeat class 69
Rule class 69
RuleReference class 69

S

sample VPAs
  Derek 96-98
  Derek, URL 96
  Jack 96-98
  Jack, URL 96
  Stacy 96-98
  Stacy, URL 96
saveXMLInString() method 50
searchCriterion attribute 43
SemanticParsing class 70
SemanticParsing object 70
SendMessage app 82, 84
SendMessage class 84
sendMessage method 82
setAckCheckBox element 84
setContactList element 84
setGrammar method 81
setListView method 30

setLocaleList() method 20
setRecognitionParams method 29
setSpeakButton() method 20
setStopButton() method 20
setUrgencyRadioGroup element 84
showDefaultValues method 29
showResults() method 58
shutdown() method 20
signal processing stage 23
SillyParrot app 76, 77
similarApps collection 41
SimpleParrot app 79
solveReferences method 70
Speak button 20
speak() method 18, 20
speech
  using, on Android device 7-10
speech app
  designing 11
  developing 11
speech recognition
  grammers, using 61
  stages 23
  stages, signal processing 23
  stages, speech recognition 23
  technology 24
  user input techniques 101
speech recognition, Google
  using 24, 25
speech recognition stage 23
SpeechRecognizer approach 25, 26
SpeechRecognizer class 31, 33
SpeechRecognizer instance 31
SpeechRecognizer object 31
speech-to-text 7, 8
src attribute 81
Stacy bot
  about 96, 97
  URL 96
startActivityForResult(Intent,int) method 27
startASR method 76
startDialog() method 57
startInterpreting() method 53
START_TAG event 52

statistical classification system
about 89
advantages 89
creating 89
disadvantage 89
statistical grammar
about 67
disadvantages 67
processing 71
types 67
statistical NLU
about 66
disadvantages 67
NLULib 68
statistical grammars, processing 71
XML grammars, processing 68-71
Stop button 20
stop() method 20
system output 101

T

template attribute 91
TEXT event 52
Text-to-speech. *See* **TTS**
TextToSpeech class 18
TextToSpeech.Engine class 18
TextToSpeech instance 19
TextToSpeech object 18
TextView box 72
threading 49, 50
Tool icon 25
TTS
about 8, 15, 16
example 8
technology 16, 17
technology, stages 16
using 15, 16
versus, pre-recorded speech 17
TTS.java class 19
TTSLib library 57
TTSReadFile app
file, reading out loud 20
screenshot 20
TTSWithIntent app 19

TTSWithLib app
screenshot 19
user input, reading 19, 20

U

UI thread 49
user input techniques
developing 101, 102
user intention
categories 90
determining 88-90
user interface 102

V

Virtual Personal Assistant. *See* **VPA**
voice interactions
about 35
advantages 36
structure, example 36
VoiceLaunch app
functionality 37, 38
screenshot 38
similarity, computing 38-42
similarity criteria, examples 39
working 40, 41
VoiceLaunch app similarities
orthographic similarity 38
phonetic similarity 39
Voice Search
about 8
example 8
feature 8
VoiceSearch app
about 36
working 36, 37
VoiceSearchConfirmation app
about 43
functionality 43
sample interactions 43
Voice User Interfaces. *See* **VUIs**
VoiceXML
URL 48
Voxeo Evolution
URL 49

VPA
  about 9, 87, 88
  approaches 98, 99
  basic requirement 13
  characteristics 10
  creating, components diagram 12
  tasks, performing 87
  user's intention, determining 88-90
VPA characteristics
  Chatbots 10
  Dialog systems 10
  ECAs 10
  VUIs 10
VPALib library
  about 94
  working 94, 95
VUIs 7 10
VXMLParser class 52

W

WEATHER_DETAILS action 67
WEATHER_STATUS action 67

X

XML grammars
  processing 68-71
XMLLib library 50, 51
XMLPullParser class 52, 68, 94

Thank you for buying
Voice Application Development for Android

About Packt Publishing

Packt, pronounced 'packed', published its first book *"Mastering phpMyAdmin for Effective MySQL Management"* in April 2004 and subsequently continued to specialize in publishing highly focused books on specific technologies and solutions.

Our books and publications share the experiences of your fellow IT professionals in adapting and customizing today's systems, applications, and frameworks. Our solution based books give you the knowledge and power to customize the software and technologies you're using to get the job done. Packt books are more specific and less general than the IT books you have seen in the past. Our unique business model allows us to bring you more focused information, giving you more of what you need to know, and less of what you don't.

Packt is a modern, yet unique publishing company, which focuses on producing quality, cutting-edge books for communities of developers, administrators, and newbies alike. For more information, please visit our website: www.packtpub.com.

About Packt Open Source

In 2010, Packt launched two new brands, Packt Open Source and Packt Enterprise, in order to continue its focus on specialization. This book is part of the Packt Open Source brand, home to books published on software built around Open Source licences, and offering information to anybody from advanced developers to budding web designers. The Open Source brand also runs Packt's Open Source Royalty Scheme, by which Packt gives a royalty to each Open Source project about whose software a book is sold.

Writing for Packt

We welcome all inquiries from people who are interested in authoring. Book proposals should be sent to author@packtpub.com. If your book idea is still at an early stage and you would like to discuss it first before writing a formal book proposal, contact us; one of our commissioning editors will get in touch with you.

We're not just looking for published authors; if you have strong technical skills but no writing experience, our experienced editors can help you develop a writing career, or simply get some additional reward for your expertise.

Android 4: New Features for Application Development

ISBN: 978-1-84951-952-6   Paperback: 166 pages

Develop Android applications using the new features of Android Ice Cream Sandwich

1. Learn new APIs in Android 4

2. Get familiar with the best practices in developing Android applications

3. Step-by-step approach with clearly explained sample codes

Instant Android Fragmentation Management How-to [Instant]

ISBN: 978-1-78216-086-1   Paperback: 66 pages

A complete hands-on guide to solving the biggest problem facing android application developers today

1. Learn something new in an instant! A short, fast, focused guide delivering immediate results.

2. Learn how to write apps that work on any Android version

3. Ready to use code to solve any compatibility issue

4. Get hands-on with the biggest issue that faces Android developers

Please check **www.PacktPub.com** for information on our titles

www.ingramcontent.com/pod-product-compliance
Lightning Source LLC
Chambersburg PA
CBHW060152060326
40690CB00018B/4076